A Good Start?
Four Year Olds in Infant Schools

A Good Start?
Four Year Olds in Infant Schools

Neville Bennett
and
Joy Kell

Blackwell Education

First published 1989

Published by
Basil Blackwell Ltd
108 Cowley Road
Oxford OX4 1JF
England

British Library Cataloguing in Publication Data

Bennett, Neville, *1937-*
   A good start? : four year olds in infant
   schools
   1. Great Britain. Infant Schools
   I. Title II. Kell, Joy
   372'.241'0941

   ISBN 0-631-16969-5
   ISBN 0-631-16971-7 Pbk

Typeset in 10/12pt Sabon
by Witwell Ltd, Southport
Printed in Great Britain
by T J Press, Padstow, Cornwall

Contents

Acknowledgements

This book reports the findings of a study jointly supported by three local education authorities. Their identity is not reported in order to maintain confidentiality. Nevertheless we express our gratitude to them since without their support the study could not have been undertaken.

The support was in the form of the full-time secondment of a head teacher of an infant, first or nursery school, usually for one school year, although one LEA was able to extend this by a term. It is to these three people – Alix Beleschenko, Ros Wheat and Joy Kell (the second author) that gratitude must particularly be expressed. They brought their experience and commitment to bear on the complex issues involved, and carried out the interviews and observations competently and conscientiously.

A special word of thanks must also be extended to the headteachers and class teachers who agreed to participate in the study, and particularly to those teachers in whose classes we observed. They gave unstintingly of their time and cooperation even when under pressure.

Two other people deserve a mention. Firstly Elisabeth Dunne, who so ably collated and analysed the interview data; and secondly, Pamela Hoad, who undertook the task of typing the drafts. This she undertook with speed, accuracy and humour even when drafts did disappearing tricks in wayward wordprocessors.

PART ONE:

Policy and practice

1 Early Admission to School: Policy and Practice

Policy

The 1944 Education Act requires that children commence full-time education in the term following their fifth birthday. This has resulted in a traditional admission pattern of three intakes per year. This is, in fact, one of the lowest ages for school admission in Europe and, as both Stretzer (1964) and Woodhead (1989) have shown, it is grounded in no clear educational rationale. After tracing the historical and political antecedents to the decision, Stretzer concluded that the age of admission was not based on any pedagogical or psychological principles but was 'the accidental result of the exigencies of Parliamentary procedure and of general unconcern!'

Nevertheless, despite enjoying the lowest school entry age in Europe, LEAs have, over several years, increasingly allowed children to enter school from the age of four years. So significant has this movement been that there are now more four year olds in infant classes than in nursery provision. The latest available figures show the extent of this movement. In 1985/86 there were nearly 440,000 children under five attending infant classes in England. This represents some 37% of the age group. In Wales over 33,000, almost half of the age group, were in infant classes, and in Northern Ireland over 45,000 attended, one third of the age group (DES, 1987a; Woodhead, 1989). The argument that there is a trend in practice, if not in statute, towards lowering the age of entry to schools seems a valid one on the basis of such figures (Sharp, 1987).

Alongside this unofficial shift in age of entry has been a change in conventional admission patterns. Sharp (1987), following on an earlier survey of LEAs by Cleave et al (1985), has shown that 37 LEAs (together with some schools in a further 19 LEAs) have an annual admission policy, allowing children entry in the year in which they become five. 13 LEAs operate a bi-annual entry, usually September and January or February, and 31 LEAs allow three intakes per year ie admitting 'rising fives'. Only 8 LEAs retained a policy of admitting at the statutory age. The pattern across the country is even more varied than these figures would indicate because 35 LEAs operate mixed policies, so that, for example, some schools admit twice yearly and others thrice yearly even though located in the same LEA.

As a consequence children's experiences of school can vary dependent on which LEA, and often in which part of an LEA, their parents happen to live. Age of admission can thus be just over four years for a child born in August and admitted in September, to five years four months, for a child born in April and admitted at the beginning of September. These discrepancies are not related in any way to the developmental maturity of the children, or their readiness to receive instruction, they are entirely a consequence of different LEA and school policies on admission (Woodhead, 1989).

A DES circular in 1975 urged LEAs not to admit children under five unless they make no additional call on educational resources and do not prevent the redeployment of these resources for more essential purposes (Osborn, 1981). So why has the move to early admissions become so significant? Woodhead (1989) argues that the trend has occurred mainly as a result of local responses to local conditions and pressures, and as such the reasons for changes in policy vary from one part of the country to the other.

One important factor has been a substantial demand for pre-school provision, a demand which has been ill-served by official ambivalence about a national pre-school policy. Although the playgroup movement has, as a consequence, grown rapidly, parents still tend to prefer their children to enter infant school rather than these alternative provisions, presumably in the belief that this will most enhance their potential for educational progress. Full-time rather than part-time attendance is also an attractive proposition for families in which both parents work, and it is, of course, free.

A further factor affecting early admissions has been the availability of space and teaching resources due to falling school rolls. In these circumstances head teachers began to expand the age range of the school to keep up their school numbers and their staffing, an expedient to which LEAs turned a blind eye. This is not surprising since early admission to infant classes provided LEAs with the opportunity not to set up nursery provision with its more expensive staffing and resource requirements.

However, it would be wrong to portray the impression that the early admission movement has been dictated entirely by expedience. The continuing move to an annual admission system has in part been driven by concern at the fate of summer-born children. Under the conventional three intake system such children experienced two terms less infant schooling, and they were always the youngest in their class. The adverse effects of this have consistently been reflected in research studies which have shown that such children perform less well in attainment tests, even through to junior and secondary school; have more difficulty in adjusting to school initially because they are breaking into existing groups where organisational procedures and friendship patterns are already established, and are treated differently by their teachers (Kellmer Pringle et al, 1966; Bookbinder, 1967; Barker Lunn, 1972; Fogelman and Gorbach, 1978; Hughes et al, 1979; Russell and Startup, 1986; Mortimore et al, 1988.)

The Select Committee Report 'Achievement in Primary Schools' (1986) reflected this concern with the summer-born child and accepted the one intake system as administratively more tidy, avoiding the termly movement that can happen in three termly intakes, and recommended

> that local education authorities should, if they do not already do so, and under suitable conditions, move towards allowing entry into the maintained education system at the beginning of the school year in which the child becomes five. We consider the conditions most likely to be suitable in a nursery school or class, but accept that admission could be to an infant class where the head teacher and parents agree to the admission.

This slight note of official scepticism about early admissions to infant classes is stressed by many, and particularly by those responsible for alternative types of provision. Thus, Lady Plowden, talking to the Pre-School Playgroup Association in 1982, strongly held that four year olds should not routinely be admitted to reception classes:

> I deplore the present practice of beheading nursery schools and playgroups by sending the four year old into the reception class of the infant school so as to fill empty spaces and no doubt keep the numbers up in the school.

This message was later re-emphasised in a joint statement from the Pre-School Playgroup Association and the British Association for Early Childhood Education.

> We regret that in deciding on a once a year entry policy, the local authorities have turned away from any consideration of children's needs to an arrangement which is mainly concerned with administrative tidiness and convenience.... Most four year olds are not ready to be confined to crowded classroom without scope for physical and imaginative play. They are still mastering physical skills for which they need opportunities not generally found in the primary classroom.
>
> (undated)

These general and specific concerns were also raised by the DES in the White Paper 'Better Schools' (1985), where it was argued that there should be sufficient regard for the maturity and readiness of children, and that teaching, ancillary staff, accommodation and resources must be appropriate to the age group. Admitting young four year olds requires a consideration of such resources as direct access to outdoor areas and an adequate number of teaching and other staff with the appropriate skills. The report averred that the curriculum offered in infant classes may not be appropriate. It is

> unrealistic to expect a teacher simultaneously to provide an appropriate education for younger four year olds and for children of compulsory school age. Very young children can be introduced too early to the more formal language and number skills and they miss the essential exploratory and practical work through which a good nursery programme forms a sound basis for teaching. Some four year old children are now moved up too early from nursery class or school, and suffer similar disadvantages.

But is such rhetoric borne out by research evidence? It is certainly the case that staffing is much more generous in nursery education because of the employment of professional nursery assistants. In 1986, for example, the ratio of children to adults in English nurseries averaged 10.7:1, whereas it was more than double that in primary classes (DES 1987 a.b.). Typical class sizes in infant schools are often nearer to 30, and cognisant of this, the Select Committee recommended that children under five should only be admitted if the total full-time equivalent number of children in the class does not exceed 26. However Sharp (1987) found that only one half of LEAs stipulated a maximum class size, and in only one third of these was the number specified as low as that recommended by the Select Committee. She also found that the majority of LEAs provided no ancillary staffing to infant classes containing four year olds. There were also marked variations in those that did, from a full-time ancillary in each class, to part-time provision if need could be demonstrated. In most infant classrooms, therefore, the level of ancillary support is inferior to that in nursery schools and classes. The Select Committee, mindful of this, recommended that there should be a full-time ancillary worker in addition to the teacher where members exceeded a suggested level, and that they should be NNEB trained.

Clark (1988) and Barrett (1986) question whether the pre-service training of teachers could have prepared them adequately for the present situation, even if they had received training appropriate to the age group. Sharp's (1987) survey indicated that most teachers of infant classes have not, in general, initially been trained to teach children under five, and that their experience with such children is very limited. In-service education is one way of overcoming such difficulties but provision has been patchy. Sharp found that it was the LEAs which had recently changed their policy to annual admission, together with those running carefully-maintained annual admission schemes, which held courses specifically for teachers of four year olds. Since this survey government funding has changed in this area and such courses have been granted national priority status. Provision should therefore increase markedly in quantity if not in quality.

Given the lack of training and experience of the infant teaching force it might be expected that LEAs would attempt to ameliorate the situation by providing curriculum guidance. Again such provision is patchy. One third of LEAs give no guidance, one quarter provide written guidance and the rest claim to provide guidance through in-service activities (Sharp, 1987).

Another area in which infant classes suffer in comparison with nurseries is in resource provision. HMI inspections have indicated that provision for four year olds suffers from inadequate resources and equipment, and both Thomas (1987) and Peel (1988) make the same claim in relation to their own LEAs. Capitation, or lack of it, is one problem since LEAs are not obliged by law to provide it, and some do not. But the utility of existing resources in infant schools is another. Peel, for example, writes of classrooms that are often too small to provide a suitable curriculum, toilets which are badly situated, floor coverings which are inappropriate, and lack of outdoor space.

That the lack of adequate resources is a widespread problem can be gauged from Sharp's survey in which two-thirds of LEAs admitted to giving no funds for the purchase of materials and equipment. Most of those that did, allocated small sums which schools had to bid for.

Practice

So what, in the face of such adversities, are infant teachers achieving with their four year olds? Not a great deal, according to official sources. Staniland (1986) outlined what HMI inspections had shown:

> Provision for four year olds in many reception classes suffers from inadequate resources and equipment, no, or reduced, capitation, staff with inappropriate training and experience, too long a day for many children and *most importantly, an inappropriate curriculum with unnecessary distinctions between work and play.*
>
> (Underlining in original)

Independent studies are few in number and of small scale but present a reasonably uniform picture. Sharp (1987) interviewed ancillary staff, teachers and head teachers in 12 schools, and followed this up with observations for one week in two classes. When asked about their aims the teachers generally expressed one major objective – to make the children's first year in school a happy one, to have them feel secure and enable them to gain some responsibility and independence. This over-arching aim is very similar to those reported by Bennett (1987) from a questionnaire survey of 58 teachers. Two statements appeared consistently – to help each child feel confident and secure, and to help each child experience a sense of achievement. These teachers rated personal qualities, attitudes to work and home-school relationships much higher than development of competence in the 3Rs, as indeed did the teachers in Sharp's study.

However, in both studies, there appeared a marked discontinuity between stated aims and practice. When Sharp asked about methods of organising the classroom and curriculum the teachers tended to concentrate their attention on reading, writing and number, and only a small proportion talked of children's engagement in play activities. When Bennett followed up with a survey of classroom organisation she found that large amounts of time were allocated to working in large groups and working on structured schemes which she felt 'may discourage appropriate attitudes to learning, self confidence and language skills'.

Sestini (1987) studied activities in both reception and nursery classes. In the former context she found that play activities served social functions and provided little evidence of cognitive challenge. The children's expectations of play were constrained not only by limited resources, space and time, but also orientation to play as a peer group social activity, not as an activity which promotes learning. Peel's (1988) preliminary findings from an evaluation in one LEA portray a similar kind of story.

Sadly, pencils and paper are too often seen as the main ingredients of the diet. Too often it is 'work' in the morning and 'play' in the afternoon, and there was a real need for teachers to consider the restrictions imposed by rigid timetables.

Although not focusing specifically on four year olds, two studies have contrasted practice in reception classes and in pre-school classes. Cleave et al (1982) found four main differences between the two:

1   The amount of dead or non-task time eg queueing, waiting, was three times as frequent in infant classes.
2   The extent to which children could choose activities was very different. It was much higher in pre-school classes. In infant classes, two thirds of the child's play was spent in carrying out specific activities selected by the teacher.
3   The distinction between work and play was more explicit in reception classes.
4   The number of children who were in direct or indirect contact was very different in the two settings.

Interestingly, two thirds of the teachers in the infant classes said they were under pressure from parents to provide a more formal curriculum, a sentiment echoed by teachers interviewed by Bennett (1987). Clark (1988) blames this on lack of communication with parents which means that many parents fail to understand the significance of the more extended aspects of the curriculum which may be seen merely as play rather than work.

The picture that emerges from the research evidence is clearly not a rosy one. It portrays inappropriately trained teachers attempting, with little assistance, to provide a differentiated curriculum to classes of some 30 children covering an age range of two or three years. Teachers are characterised as having honourable intentions but without the experience, resources or parental support to carry them out. They thus fall back on stressing the 3Rs, thereby denying the four year olds the curriculum they need and deserve.

But how fair a picture is this? These interpretations and evaluations of infant practice are of course based on assumptions about what is better, or more acceptable, provision. And it is clear from official accounts what that provision ought to be. The DES document *Better Schools* makes it clear that 'a good nursery programme forms a sound basis for later learning', and the Select Committee filled in the detail of that programme with the dictum 'the education of young children is founded in play'. These views have been reinforced by HMI, who at the same time have raised the important question of whether the ideal is actually being met in nurseries. Staniland (1986) for example, asked whether, through play, nurseries are giving sufficient attention to progression, challenge and reflection. And Weir (1988) makes it clear that in his view play is not intended to provide a panacea for shapeless, laissez-faire activity, arguing that it requires imaginative interpretation and an agreed professional commitment not easily achieved or recognised. What is needed, he concluded, is more clarity about how play builds into a curriculum of high calibre.

The limited amount of research on pre-school education would seem to bear out those concerns regarding the nature and utility of play activities. It will be recalled that Sestini (1987) found that play in reception classes lacked cognitive challenge. Peer play in nurseries also remained at a low level unless there was adult participation. Sylva et al (1980) also found that older pre-school children found play most stimulating with an adult. However, it was also reported that frequent adult questions tended to generate monosyllabic responses, and adult talk in general was limited to the 'here and now'. Both studies implied that more challenging play opportunities were needed.

A similar view was voiced by Hutt et al (1984). They claimed that environments in pre-school are structured to encourage ludic rather than epistemic play, ie behaviour for self amusement, less focused, and mood dependent, rather than concerned with the acquisition of knowledge. They stress that epistemic play is necessary for learning and requires a good adult-child ratio to enable the appropriate communication. They found, as did Sylva et al, that there was little evidence of complex conversation with children, or discussion of past and future events. Instead attempts were made to respond to all children resulting in superficial exchanges with some children rarely involved. Sand, water and fantasy play were often limited and repetitive.

This portrayal is supported by Cashdan and Meadows (1983) from observations of practice in pre-school units. They found that although play could be interesting and purposeful, it was often brief and repetitive, lacking in complexity and social participation. There was little evidence of sustained or uninterrupted conversation between children and adults. Cashdan and Meadows were thus forced to question, in conclusion, whether an ideology of free play and non-interventionist adults is an environment providing sufficient intellectual challenge.

Other observers of the pre-school scene have posed similar questions. Hughes et al (1980), for example, offered the conclusion that 'ordinary nursery education, with its emphasis on free play, does not generally produce gains', and there is accumulating evidence of the underestimation of young children's cognitive skills in pre-school provision (cf Bruner, 1980; Hughes 1983; Sestini, 1987; Thomas, 1987).

Clark's (1988) view that 'it is dangerous to assume that early entry to primary school gives children a good start' could, on the basis of the evidence above, be equally applied to pre-school. It would seem from the above that although early childhood educators have an idea of what should constitute a good quality nursery experience (cf Curtis, 1987) they cannot yet adequately deliver it. The findings considered so far thus give few grounds for confidence in either type of provision, and could hardly be used as the basis of guidance to parents. And unfortunately comparative studies of the different forms of provision are of little help. Typical of these is the recent study by Osborn and Milbank (1987). They focused on type of provision rather than on practice within provision and as a consequence their findings are difficult to interpret. They claim that playgroups have the greatest influence on later achievement, that nursery schools have a higher than average effect, but that nursery classes have a lower than average effect. They further claim that children starting infant school before 4 years 5 months had the highest average reading score at age ten, and 'rising fives' the lowest. Unfortunately there is no way of explaining such findings because of lack of data on processes. The conclusion of relevance here, however, is that 'we found no conclusive or consistent evidence to suggest that there was any educational or behavioural advantage or disadvantage for children who entered infant reception classes before the statutory age'.

Weir (1988), as befits a senior HMI, clearly wishes to move the discussion on. He is less concerned about where four year olds are educated then how, ie for making good provision for four year olds wherever they are. There should be less concern for location and more consideration of well-differentiated provision and how best to match curriculum to the identified and individual needs of children. However, after studying the literature in this field, it is clear that Weir is a hare among hounds. There is precious little indication that the argument about location is ended, or that there is a thriving and thoughtful debate about such crucial issues as how to achieve differentiation, how to identify or diagnose children's needs, or what progression might look like in a pre-school or reception class. This debate ought to be linked to research which, as Clark (1988) has indicated, should focus its attention on the content and quality of the provision rather than, as has tended to happen in the past, on coordination and organisational aspects. Only then, she argues, can features which are important to children's development be identified and the insights from research be fully reflected in the pre- and in-service training of teachers. The study reported here is one step in that direction.

2 The School and Classroom Context

It is apparent from the consideration of previous studies that the debate about the what and where of the education of four year olds is proceeding largely in the absence of knowledge of actual practice. So basic questions such as: what is the nature and content of the activities that four year olds typically engage in? what proportion are self-chosen rather than imposed? to what extent are they appropriate or differentiated? simply cannot be answered.

A major aim of this study was to shed some light on these issues by observing children and their classroom activities through one term of their first year in school. A second aim was to provide the necessary context for these observations by acquiring information on those LEA, school, and classroom policies which bear directly or indirectly on pupils' classroom experiences. The study was therefore designed in two linked stages. In the first the head teacher and at least one teacher teaching four year olds were interviewed in 60 schools, 20 schools in each of three LEAs. The interviews were followed by observations of children in six of those same 20 schools, ie 18 schools in total. These observations are considered in Chapter Four.

The three LEAs selected each had a different intake policy; one had an annual intake, one a bi-annual, and the third a termly intake pattern. In each LEA a sample of 20 schools was chosen to reflect as adequately as possible different types, sizes and catchment areas. Infant and first schools were considered as one type, as were primary and combined. Three broad categories of size were used, larger, medium and smaller. Smaller schools were defined as those with three teachers or less; medium schools employed four to seven teachers; and larger schools more than eight teachers.

It was not possible to acquire a perfect match across LEAs simply because of the differing geographical and demographical factors at work in each authority. For example some had many more small, or large, schools than others, and different patterns of intake. Identical numbers of infant/first and primary/combined schools were achieved but with a predominance of larger schools, as Table 2.1 shows.

Table 2.1 Size and type of school sample

TYPE	SIZE			
	Smaller	*Medium*	*Larger*	*Total*
Infant/First	6	9	15	30
Primary/Combined	7	7	16	30
TOTAL	13	16	31	60

As indicated above, each head teacher and at least one teacher were interviewed in each school. Consequently 60 head teachers and 71 teachers were sampled. The interviews were structured, so that the same information could be acquired from each participant, but the schedule itself contained a mixture of closed and open questions. The closed questions were used for factual information, eg how long have you been teaching this age group?, and the open questions were used for more complex areas such as aims and classroom practice. In this way the interviewees could respond in any manner they desired without the imposition of an arbitrary framework by the research team.

The interview schedules were developed and piloted on the bases of previous studies, visits to schools, talking to teachers and advisers and, not least, drawing on the extensive experience of the three seconded head teachers who carried out the interviews and observations. One was a very experienced head of a medium sized infant school, another was the head of a first school, and the third the head of a nursery unit. The schedules can be seen in Appendix A on page 137.

The interviews were carried out in the Autumn term and were either recorded in long hand or tape-recorded for later transcription and analysis. The information derived from the interviews is presented in five sections – intake policy, resources, philosophy, classroom processes, and perceived problems. This order allows the reader to gain some knowledge of the LEA context before considering the school context, which in turn precedes a consideration of aims and processes in the classroom.

Intake policy

The three LEAs were chosen because each had a different intake policy. LEA A has a one intake policy allowing admission to children whose birthday falls within the school year. Thus children as young as 4 years 1 month attend infant classes. Initially these are part-time, either five half days or three full days, dependent on transport. They become full time in the term in which they become five years old, ie 'rising fives'. Certain restrictions are imposed by the LEA. For example, such children should not be placed with a probationary teacher, and not with a class of more than three years range and/or a class size above 30.

LEA **B** has a policy of admitting at three points in the year – September, January and April. All entry is full time. The age range admitted is therefore narrower than in **A**, from 4 years 8 months to 4 years 11 months, ie only 'rising fives'. Some schools do admit children younger than this but this contravenes LEA policy.

LEA **C** has a two intake pattern, admitting in September and February, ie entering children from four and a half years old. LEA policy is that children initially enter part-time but in reality head teachers are left with a wide measure of discretion. Some schools keep their intake part-time for a term, some for half a term, others for a few weeks. Some had abandoned the official policy altogether and admitted the children as full time from the first day of entry.

It is evident from these sketches that LEA policy presents a general context within which head teachers operate with some discretion. Intake practice therefore varies across LEAs and within LEAs. So what did head teachers think of the policy they had to implement?

In **A** they voiced much approval. Only one of the 20 head teachers interviewed actually showed disapproval. They did however take the opportunity to argue for more full-time auxiliary assistance, and one fifth of them called for nursery provision in each school.

In **B** nearly one half of the heads approved of the present system provided that class sizes could be kept at a reasonable level. However, over a third stated a preference for a two-intake system, and a further ten percent wanted an annual entry.

In **C**, on the other hand, there was near universal condemnation of their two intake policy, nearly one half wanting an annual entry.

In other words, there was in two LEAs a tendency to want each other's system. Many heads in the two intake system wanted an annual intake, whilst a sizeable number of those operating a three entry system wanted two entry points.

School policies on intake procedures varied widely. Most schools claimed to encourage visits to school by the parents and children, both individually and in groups. A majority also claimed to liaise with local playgroups. Home visiting was patchy and varied greatly from LEA to LEA. In **B** one half of the head teachers claimed to visit the home whereas in **A** only five percent did so.

Variability was also apparent in the manner in which children are grouped on arrival in school. Mixed age classes predominated, particularly in LEAs **B** and **C**, which had 85 per cent and 69 per cent of their reception classes in mixed age form. Nevertheless, attempts appear to have been made to keep the age range low, as can be seen in Table 2.2.

It is apparent from the table that a majority of children in each LEA were placed in a class which contained children no more than one year older. There were of course exceptions. In one school the age range was 5.2 years, but the widest age ranges tended to be in the region of 2.5–2.7 years.

Intakes to schools obviously varied and children therefore found themselves in classrooms with very different numbers of fellow four year olds. An indication of

Table 2.2 Age ranges in classes in each LEA

	Age range	% classes
LEA A	4.1 – 5.1	64
	4.1 – 6.1	32
	4.1 – 7.1	3
LEA B	4.8 – 4.11	35
	4.8 – 5.8	55
	4.8 – 6.8	5
	4.8 – 10.0	5
LEA C	4.6 – 5.0	68
	4.6 – 5.6	8
	4.6 – 6.0	8
	4.6 – 6.9	16

this variablity can be gained from the range in each LEA. In **A** it ranged from 2 to 23 children, in **B** from 5 to 35, and in **C** from 1 to 22.

The children also experienced different degrees of disruption in their early school careers. Many found themselves changing class, and changing teacher, at some stage in their first year, requiring new relationships to be formed, new expectations to learn and a new group to be socialised into.

The size of classes varied widely, although the head teachers' belief that 20 was an ideal size was in general realised in the Autumn term. Later intakes suffered larger class sizes in addition to the likelihood of being taught by a new, and probably temporary, teacher. The difficulties of appointing teachers with appropriate experience midway through the year was in fact a constant source of concern to head teachers, and it is to the human and material resources in the schools that we now turn.

Resources

Teachers are of course the most important resource in a school, but a resource which critics of four year old education in infant classes have subjected to much criticism. We therefore ascertained the training and experience of the 71 teachers interviewed in the three authorities. The findings are shown in Table 2.3.

For example, the top line shows that five of the 71 teachers had between no and five years experience overall, but that 25 of the 71 had less than five years experience teaching reception classes. One half of them, ie 35 of 71, had less than five years experience teaching four year olds.

What the table shows overall is that the teachers interviewed were very experienced in general but few had long experience of teaching four year olds. Four

Table 2.3 Teacher experience

Years experience	Total	Reception	Four year olds
0 – 5	5	25	35
6 – 10	19	25	11
11 – 20	31	16	10
21 – 30	8	1	–
31 – 40	7	2	1
Range	2 – 40	1 – 40	1 – 35

of the teachers had no previous experience teaching reception class, and a further four had had no previous experience teaching four year olds.

A similar story can be written of their training, details of which are presented in Table 2.4. This shows that 18 of 71, ie only one quarter, of those teaching four year olds had actually been trained for that age range.

Table 2.4 Teachers' training

Age range trained for	No. of teachers
3 – 7	18
5 – 8	16
5 – 11	26
7 – 12	7
11 – 16	4

When asked about their teaching preferences, four of the 18 did not prefer teaching this age group. In other words, less than one fifth of teachers are both trained for, and prefer, teaching this group of children.

Financial provision

It was clear from Sharp's survey that LEAs varied in the manner in which they provided capitation, and this general picture is reflected in the differing policies in the three authorities studied. The concern here, however, is less with LEA than school policy. What teachers are concerned about is the extent of the resources at their disposal for teaching purposes. As such head teachers were asked if there was any particular financial provision made specifically for four year olds; if so, what was it? and where did it come from?

Over one third admitted that no specific funding was available for this age group, most making provision as and where the need appeared in the school as a whole.

However, one in eight did say that no provision at all was available. The rest made specific amounts available to the teachers who then decided on how it should be spent. This was allocated either by the head sharing the resources, equally or unequally, across the staff, by teachers bidding for a share, or by the staff as a whole coming to a joint decision about amounts to be allocated.

Head teachers in general were very coy about putting a number to this provision, but more telling perhaps is that only four of the 60 interviewed gave the highest financial priority to this group.

When asked where the resources came from, heads indicated that three quarters came from capitation and school funding. The remainder came from a variety of outlets including new head teachers allowance, new school setting up allowances, some community funding and various entrepreneurial efforts including local trusts and banks.

The head teachers' claim that teachers were actually consulted was borne out by the teachers themselves. Three quarters reckoned to have been consulted, but not all were thereby satisfied, as Table 2.5 shows:

Table 2.5 Consultation and satisfaction among teachers (% rounded)

	Satisfied	Not satisfied	Total
Consulted	33	40	73
Not consulted	9	17	26
Total	42	57	100

Three quarters of teachers had been consulted but nearly 60 percent were dissatisfied with the outcome. There were, however, substantial differences between LEAs. Eighty percent of teachers in LEA B were dissatisfied compared with only one third in LEA C, and this was the same irrespective of school size or location.

The resources which teachers most frequently stated they needed were large construction toys and equipment, and other large play objects such as sand and water trays, dolls' prams, play houses and puppet theatres. Some outside play equipment was also called for. Next in order of priority came pre-number and practical maths equipment, games and puzzles, books, and art and craft materials. In one authority they complained of inadequate furniture, including chairs and trays.

The demand for additional large equipment and play apparatus is somewhat ironic, for, as will be seen below, many teachers also complained of lack of space.

Space

Space is a critical requirement for adequate teaching, but many teachers felt they had insufficient, particularly in the Summer term. Satisfaction with space in the Summer term fell to one quarter in one authority, and even in the best-resourced LEA, less than half of the teachers felt they had adequate space by the end of the year. The space that was available was, by and large, either a single room or two rooms shared with another teacher.

Nevertheless, teachers were reasonably happy with such facilities as display, practical areas, quiet areas, carpeting and water supply. There was, however, a noticeable difference in the provision of these facilities across the three authorities.

There were more difficulties with access to facilities outside the classroom. One third of teachers complained of poor access to toilets and outdoor play areas. Difficulty of access to cloakrooms was also mentioned by 20 percent of them. Problems of access seemed acute in small schools. Small schools also suffered more from lack of auxiliary help.

Auxiliary and parental help

The patterns of auxiliary (or ancillary) help across the three authorities were quite bewildering. Schools in the same LEA enjoyed different levels of support, and for different periods of the week, and the three authorities provided quite different levels of support to their schools. For example, in LEA A, the best provider, the range of auxiliary support in average sized primary schools varied from six to 25 hours per week, and was available from three to five days per week, a pattern which in part reflected head teacher decisions on provision within schools. In another authority several schools got no support whatsoever, and those tended to be small schools. The averages in the three authorities are shown in Table 2.6 by size of school:

Table 2.6 Availability of auxiliary support

| | School size | | | Range | | |
LEA	Small	Medium	Large	Days	Hours	Av. Hours
A	100%	100%	100%	2 – 5	5 – 25	15.8
B	17%	100%	100%	0 – 5	0 – 15	6.2
C	100%	100%	81%	0 – 5	0 – 15	5.0

The table presents a fairly dismal picture overall, but particularly in LEAs **B** and C, each of which provides an average of about one hour per day per class, whereas LEA A provides three times that. Interestingly, but not perhaps surprisingly, least parental help is available in the LEA which provides most paid auxiliary support. Thus in LEA A slightly less than half the schools enjoy parental help, whereas in the others over 80 percent do so. The kind of help also varied markedly in frequency and duration. But in schools which did receive parental help it was consistent in each authority at around six hours per week. Table 2.7 shows how teachers use the help provided by auxiliaries and parents.

Table 2.7 *Auxiliary and parental help (% rounded)*

Area	Auxiliaries	Parents
Pre-language/maths	70	40
Materials	66	32
Art and crafts	56	51
Domestic care	54	15
Reading	38	34
Home Economics	32	51
Imaginative play/talk	25	17

The patterns of auxiliary and parent use are somewhat different. Auxiliaries are used most in pre-language and number activities and in the preparation of materials, whereas the two areas where teachers say they use parents most is in art and craft and home economics. Interestingly, the domestic care of children, dressing, toileting etc, is left to the auxiliary far more than to the parents. It is perhaps noteworthy, in the light of previous research, that imaginative talk and play is not an area rated highly by teachers for support.

So far the support structures for teaching have been considered, but what of teaching itself? What philosophies of teaching four year olds do these teachers have, and what curriculum and classroom organisations do they engender?

Philosophy

An identical question was asked of heads and teachers concerning their particular philosophy regarding the eduction of four year olds, and whether or not they felt they were able to implement it. These questions were open-ended to allow maximum flexibility of response. Responses were then grouped into broad categories for ease of description.

Three broad categories were discerned from teachers' responses, which were labelled *Affective, Cognitive* and *Preparatory*. About a half of all responses were in the Affective category. The two most popular statements here were 'to enable children to develop confidence and be happy', and 'for them to develop a caring attitude within a safe environment' – aims very similar to those reported by Sharp (1987) and Bennett (1987). About three quarters of all the statements could be fitted into these two overarching aims, indicating clearly the importance the teachers attached to them.

Other popular aims included the development of childrens' general potential, and for children to become self-reliant, independent and self disciplined. Interestingly, only one teacher aimed to enable her children to learn to work alongside each other, reflecting perhaps that teachers of this age group are more concerned with individualistic rather than group goals.

Forty percent of all responses were in the Cognitive category. Here the two most frequently occurring statements were 'to allow children to learn through first hand experience/discovery, and 'to provide an environment which will stimulate and nurture their interests'. The necessity of learning through play was also frequently mentioned, as was the necessity to provide a balance between active learning on the one hand and paper and pencil work on the other. Finally, several teachers contended that standards should be set early and that children should be given pride in their achievements.

The third, and by far the smallest, category has been labelled Preparatory. In it teachers reminded us that children must be integrated into the life and routines of the school, and be prepared for the future expectations of schooling.

When asked whether they were able to implement their philosophies, 80 percent said that they felt they were, despite the constraints of space, assistance, resources and numbers. In other words one teacher in five appears to be frustrated in their attempts to achieve their aims.

The categorisation of head teachers' statements revealed two identical categories – Affective and Cognitive, with another specifically concerned with School organisation. Their priorities were also different. One half of the head teachers' statements were in the Cognitive category, with the Affective category containing a little less than a third, and School organisation a little less than a quarter, of all responses.

Perhaps surprisingly, priority in the Cognitive area was given to the paramount importance of play in learning; surprising because few head teachers were early years specialists, and therefore might have been giving a stereotyped response. They did, however, also state clearly a belief in active learning based on first-hand experience, but unlike the teachers this was aligned with the need for assessment and diagnosis of learning – a feature not represented at all in teachers' statements. Active learning was also to be balanced with more formal learning in the head teachers' view. Other aspects given some priority were the necessity for individual attention, the need for a broad curriculum and the centrality of language development. This latter issue was also not represented in the teachers' responses which is somewhat unexpected, given the importance attached to it in early years education.

In the Affective area, the most frequent aim was that children should be happy and secure, not unlike the teachers' priority. The development of social skills in a caring community was stressed and being integrated into the school as a community.

In the School organisation category were statements reflecting head teachers' concerns that four year olds should be in a separate class with a specific curriculum, qualified helpers and proper resource provision, and that the most appropriate form of school provision was that provided in nursery classes. Not all agreed with this of course. One specifically argued that it was not right to put such children into a nursery environment, and another felt that that children settle best in an established vertically grouped class. Other statements reflected concern about transition arrangements between home and school and that part-time attendance was probably the best alternative. Finally, five of the head teachers aimed to educate those parents who appear to have pre-conceived ideas about children's progress and inappropriately apply pressure for reading and arithmetic for four year olds.

When asked if it was possible to implement their aims, 80 percent felt that they could, despite the obvious constraints, because of good staff and parental help. One in five could not implement their aims because of understaffing, underfunding and lack of space.

However, one of the clear trends to emerge from previous studies has been inconsistency of aims and actual practice, and it is to classroom processes that we now turn.

Classroom processes

Grouping

Most teachers group their children. Only three of those interviewed claimed not to. The basis on which they grouped them varied considerably, and this also varied across time and classroom activity. The most popular criterion at the time of the interviews in the Autumn term was ability, used by a little over half the teachers. This was introduced slowly over the term however, after they got to know the children. A little over a third of teachers used age or intake, and a similar proportion claimed to use flexible grouping. One in four said they used mixed ability groups, and one in six used friendship grouping.

The reality was more complex than these averages indicate since many teachers used more than one criterion. In one LEA, for example, a third of the teachers based their groups on both age and ability.

The issue of grouping is also complicated in mixed age classes by teachers' attempts to integrate the four year olds with the rest of the class. The differing ways in which teachers attempted to achieve this can be judged from the following examples:

Initially grouped according to age. As they settle and their individual needs become more apparent they may change groups. At first they have freedom of choice. This becomes more structured as they develop.

Fairly flexible grouping. Younger children spend a lot of their time in loose friendship groups or playing alongside other children, rather than cooperating in groups. But I have more formal groups when doing maths, language and pre-reading skills and activities ... (it is) easier to teach and more economical to group by ability for certain more formal activities.

The older children look after the younger ones for friendship and social development, the older ones 'teach' the younger ones board games etc.

When the children are not integrated into the rest of the class, as for example in a vertically grouped class of four to seven year olds in small schools, teachers most commonly said that the needs of each child are considered individually.

Curriculum

Teachers were asked, in an open-ended question, about their curricular priorities. Their responses were classified into five broad categories: cognitive development, general cognitive skills, play, general motor skills and affective development. Play was categorised separately since it was not always possible to tell, from what teachers said, the purpose of the play. Table 2.8 sets out the responses.

Table 2.8 Curriculum priorities (% rounded)

Cognitive development		%
i	Pre-reading and reading – includes stories, rhymes, games etc	73
ii	Pre-number and number – includes practical work, matching, counting, sorting etc	55
iii	Language development – oracy	37
iv	Creative/aesthetic – art and craft, role-play, drama, observational drawing etc	32
v	Listening skills	23
vi	Writing, handwriting	9
vii	Music, singing	4
	Play	19
Affective development		
i	Social skills, awareness, independence, expectations of school, sharing etc	35
ii	Happiness, enjoyment, positive attitudes	15
iii	Confidence, in self and others	4
General motor skills		
i	Gross and fine motor skills through all activity	15
ii	Physical control/awareness via PE, dance etc	9
iii	Manipulative skills, dexterity, hand-eye etc	7
General cognitive skills		
i	Building concentration, thinking out instructions etc	3

It will be clear from Table 2.8 that here too there is a clear discrepancy between teachers' statements of aims and their statements of curriculum priority. There has been a clear turn round in the priorities for the cognitive and affective areas, and even within these areas the priorities do not match, eg happiness and confidence are relegated below social skills in the affective area.

And how is this curriculum organised in the classroom? A general question on how children's experiences and activities were structured elicited talk of integrated day, structured activities and individualised learning which was clearly based on differing implicit definitions of those terms, and as a consequence tables of response frequencies would provide a worthless and misleading picture. Instead the following quotations have been selected to provide a flavour of the range of strategies adopted:

'An integrated day generally – a combination of class, group and individual work. I tend to put more emphasis on language, maths and science in the morning and craft work in the afternoon. The four year olds work to the same kind of pattern but their "work" time tends to be for shorter periods and their free choice time tends to be more.'

'The children structure their own day, choosing activities out of those available. Certain work has to be done each day.'

'I have basically a thematic structure. I plan a term and then have weekly planning with built-in spontaneity.'

'An integrated day. I have a choosing board and the children select from the activities that are on offer – in tune with the nursery approach.'

'We are project based each half term. We make a chart of spin-offs in each area of the curriculum. Curriculum areas are included in the project chart or planned separately – for example, the reading scheme. We keep a check list. Number work fits into the project.'

'I use reading and maths schemes as the bones of the programme. We have a theme at the same time, stories are brought in. We use our own and children's creativity. I keep records of work covered. We use a writing scheme.'

Differentiated curriculum

The term differentiation is usually used in the context of providing tasks and activities suitable to the different capabilities of children in the same class. It is to an extension of that same basic issue that the term is applied here, that is, the content and the quality of the curriculum experienced by different intakes of children into the same class. This raises several important questions such as: can later entrants possibly have the same curriculum experience as earlier entrants? If not, what elements are missed, and what effect is this likely to have? And what effect does attempting to provide parallel experiences have on the teacher?

The teachers in the two LEAs which did not have a single intake were asked about these issues. When asked how they coped with the scope of the curriculum for children who only have one, or two, terms of reception class, most admitted that it simply was not possible, and that various implications flowed from this, not least the pressure that they themselves experienced. The following quotations are representative of the range of responses made. First are those from LEA C which had two intakes per year:

'I go as far as I can, as far as their ability allows. The second intake doesn't get as much.'

'We resist choosing one part of the programme, or pushing harder. We give them the same foundations. They have the same ideas, the same standard of teaching and the same basic work, but not the same length, so they are disadvantaged.'

'Unfortunately the second intake have a condensed programme, or miss something out. Activities will not be done in the same depth. We try to go as far as possible and cover the essentials but do less of the programme.'

'We can't go back to the beginning and do "Autumn" and "hibernation"!'

Teachers in LEA B had to cope with three intakes:

In the Easter and Summer terms the children are given the same kinds of activities but they are abridged slightly – I can't go into so much depth or reinforcement. You're very much under pressure at the end of the year.

'I just get on with it – faster, although I realise that some children may not be mature or prepared enough to cope with the second year.'

'Invariably there will be disadvantages in the summer as children will be in a much larger class. They do miss out simply because they get two terms less schooling, and if they are very poor and immature they never catch up. I do feel pressurised – these children must miss out, especially in the reading scheme.'

'. . . if there's a good home background I'm not so worried.'

More teachers in this latter authority spontaneously mentioned pressure brought about particularly by the summer intake when the class sizes are at their maximum and where, in this LEA at least, there is no guarantee of additional staffing. Also more ways of alleviating the problems were suggested. The policies which had been implemented in the schools included keeping the summer intake with the same teachers until Christmas, keeping the same children together for four terms, and spending the first two years with the same teacher by utilising parallel classes. Teachers in small schools also felt that their structure had something to offer. One teacher argued

'I don't have a programme as such as each child is usually with us from rising five to eleven. Their education continues uninterrupted through the school. Continuity is good; having only two teachers we know exactly what each other has covered.'

Head teachers were asked a similar question – 'Is there any difference in the quality of educational experience the children receive in each of the intake terms?' Two-thirds gave a categorical 'Yes'. The reasons included larger class sizes, lack of time to catch up to their older peers, lack of staff and resources. The following comments illustrate these difficulties:

'In the first school you have to take on temporary part-time teachers at different times of the year. It's wrong.'

'I'm only allocated 0.5 of a teacher for the summer intake of 20 children, and that was only after a lot of hassle and letter writing from myself and the parents.'

'The quality of teaching for the second intake may not be the same; you haven't got the range of teachers to choose from.'

Others were more sanguine, claiming that care and good quality teaching could overcome such problems:

'We try to ensure there is no difference. The time factor is the major thing. The programme for the second intake is the same ... you have to try and push them through quicker to a comparable standard to the next class.'

'There is a build-up of pressure on the teacher as the year goes on – the summer term being very outdoor-oriented with swimming, sports etc. It is incumbent on the teacher to make up for the short-fall when she is more tired at the end of the year, but has to work hard with the summer intake, larger class, less space. But hopefully there is no difference because we concentrate on the quality of learning.'

Problems

Heads were asked finally if the education of four year olds created a problem in their schools. They were equally split, one half saying 'Yes' or 'Not really', and the other half 'No'. The heads who were able to answer 'No' tended to justify their response in one of the following ways:

- they had the right staff
- they were not pressurised by numbers
- these children created no more problems than any other age range, or their children started part-time

One head teacher was able to say that far from being a problem, 'in fact it's a delight'.

Those responding negatively most frequently cited lack of qualified teaching and ancillary staff, particularly in January and April, over-large classes, lack of space or other restrictions imposed by the building. There was also a case for more in-service courses for both teachers and ancillaries and for a more informed official LEA attitude to the education of four year olds. One head argued that 'I don't think the LEA has ever really appreciated the problem of the under five child', another that 'If the under fives are in school they should be better resourced', and finally, 'I think the system is going wrong at the moment. These children are simply being regarded as statutory school age before their time.'

The teachers were not asked if teaching four year olds was a problem, rather an attempt was made to gain a clear idea of the problems as perceived by them. An open-ended question produced many responses which, after analysis, were classified into four categories – school organisation, classroom management, curriculum and parents. The first two of these categories contained the bulk of the comments.

The number one problem in school organisation was the lack of a full-time, trained assistant, mentioned by over a third of teachers. Number two was the difficulties raised by the wide age range the teachers often had to deal with in mixed age classes, often exacerbated by having to cater for the different needs of full- and part-time attenders. Other important issues raised were lack of, or restriction in, space; over-large classes, particularly in the summer term; and a lack of material and equipment resources.

In classroom management terms, the greatest difficulty was caused by the children's needs for individual attention allied with the lack of time adequately to provide it. Other problems prominent in their comments related to language development. Teachers found it hard to get children to listen and follow instructions, and difficulties were also created by the children's lack of communication skills or by speech problems. Of similar importance to the problems of language were children's lack of abilities in personal skills such as dressing. Problems less frequently mentioned included the level of noise in the classroom, development of peer relationships, short attention spans, toileting, children settling down, lack of motor skills and general messiness.

Issues in the categories of curriculum and parents were few in number, if not in importance. In the former two main problems were apparent: the amount of preparation time needed, and difficulties in judging the suitability and appropriateness (ie matching) of activities. In the parents' category concern was expressed at parental pressure for progress in the basics and, following from that, the necessity to educate parents.

Summary

The three LEAs were chosen for this study because of their differing intake policies. What the interviews made clear, however, is that these policies simply provide a framework within which head teachers feel free to make decisions relevant to local circumstances. As such there is no clear pattern of school intake policies either between or within authorities. Despite this, some general issues did arise.

Few teachers in these authorities were trained for, or are experienced in, the teaching of four year olds, and most are dissatisfied with the general level of resourcing of their teaching, including equipment, materials, space, access and, most critically, the lack of full-time, trained ancillaries.

It also became apparent that there is a gulf between the aims they wish to pursue and what they attempt to achieve. Affective aims dominated their philosophy but cognitive activities dominated their curriculum. Why this should be is not totally clear, but some of the reasons are no doubt the difficulties and stress involved in attempting to deliver a differentiated curriculum in classes of sometimes wide age range, containing children with generally low levels of language and personal skills, and differential experience of school, without adequate resources and assistance, whilst feeling under pressure from parents to achieve progress in the basics. Not, perhaps, an ideal environment for the early education of the nation's progeny.

3 Observing Classroom Activities

The message from the teachers and their heads is not a heartening one. Indeed it could alarm some. Nevertheless teachers have a long record of achieving notable successes in less than ideal teaching contexts. Descriptions of teachers' perceptions and attitudes therefore need to be placed alongside descriptions and analyses of what the children themselves experience on a day-to-day basis. For this purpose extensive observations of two children in each of 18 classes, ie six schools per LEA, were carried out. This report concentrates on the 12 schools in LEAs A and C, since the observations in LEA B had a somewhat different focus.

The most critical question in any observation study is simply stated: 'What should (and should not) be observed?' There are literally hundreds of behaviours, activities and features in classrooms that can be described, and as a consequence observations have to be guided by a clear statement of purpose. The purpose of this study was, following the concerns apparent and expressed in Chapters One and Two, to ascertain the nature and quality of the learning experiences of four year old children in infant classes. And, since a further aim was to seek improvements should they be necessary, the purposes of the study also included the identification of those aspects of teaching which served to maintain that quality. But a clear statement of purpose begs more questions. What is meant by 'nature', 'quality', or 'aspects of teaching'? Answers to these questions requires a brief dip into theory.

Our approach to the study of children's classroom learning experiences is presented in detail elsewhere (cf Bennett et al, 1984; Bennett, 1988; Bennett and Desforges, 1988). Basically our approach to learning is constructivist in origin, deriving from insights provided by cognitive psychology. In this conception learners are active and interpretive, and learning is a covert, intellectual process providing the development and re-structuring of existing conceptual schemes. As such teaching effects learning through pupil thought processes, ie teaching influences pupil thinking; pupil thinking mediates learning.

Intended classroom learning is embedded in the curriculum tasks or activities that teachers present to children (or allow them to choose), and as such the activities of the learner on such tasks are crucial to their development. Thus, in order to understand classroom learning, it is necessary to observe children's performances on their tasks, and to ascertain the extent to which the demand in their assigned or chosen work is appropriate or matched to their capabilities. Also, since learning takes place in complex social settings it is necessary to assess the impact of social processes, such as grouping arrangements, peer exchanges, and adult-child interactions, on children's classroom experiences.

Our recent studies on infant classes (Bennett et al, 1984) mixed and single age junior classes (Bennett et al, 1987) and on primary and secondary age children transferring from special to ordinary schools (Bennett and Cass, 1989) have all adopted a similar focus which can be summarised by the model presented in Figure 3.1.

Classroom task processes

Teaching is, we argue, a purposeful activity: teachers provide tasks and activities for their children for good reasons. These reasons or, as we call them in the model, teacher intentions, will inform the teacher's selection of tasks/activities. Once chosen these are presented to children in some way, eg to individuals, groups or the whole class, together with the necessary materials. The children then get on with their work, demonstrating, through their performances, their understanding (or misconceptions) of it. When they have completed their activity it might be expected that the teacher will assess it in some way in order to judge children's developing competencies, and it might also be expected that the information gained from those assessments will inform the teacher's next intentions.

This model is deceptively simple however. Our previous studies have clearly

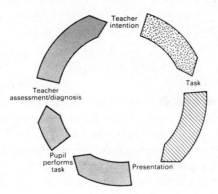

Fig 3.1: A model of classroom task processes

shown the complexities of classrooms by indicating that mismatches can, and do, occur between every element of the model. A brief overview of these is provided below in order to provide an insight into our choice of observational variables for this study.

Teacher intentions

Information on teacher purposes or intentions has rarely been acquired in previous research on teaching, yet without such information there is no basis on which to determine whether the tasks actually performed by pupils were those intended by the teacher. We have found that although teachers are clear in their intentions for their tasks, no assumption can be made about the correspondence between task and intention. In our infant school study, we observed over 600 tasks in mathematics and language activities and found that over one-fifth of the tasks did not actually meet the teacher's intentions. A typical example of a mismatch between intention and task was where teachers intended to introduce new knowledge or skills to high-attaining children, but, when the task was actually observed, it was clear that the pupils were already perfectly familiar with that knowledge or skill. As such a teacher intention for development actually turned out to be one demanding consolidation via the practice of knowledge or skills already acquired.

Presentation

A mismatch between task and presentation can occur either through lack of clarity, inadequate explanation, a lack of necessary resource materials, or differences between what the teacher asks for and what he or she assesses. A common example of the latter in our studies was in children's writing tasks where teacher demand for a really exciting and imaginative story was often assessed on length, neatness and grammar. This did not fool the children however, who consistently provided a page of neat writing with appropriate full stops and capital letters. Presentation can thus aid or hinder pupil performance, and at worst the child can actually perform a different task from that intended by the teacher.

Task appropriateness

The mismatch between classroom tasks and pupils' capabilities is the aspect of classroom practice which has most concerned Her Majesty's Inspectorate, an issue earlier defined by the Plowden Report (1967) as avoiding 'The twin pitfalls of demanding too much and expecting too little'. In their *Primary School Survey* (1978) HMI complained that teachers were tending to underestimate the higher attainers in the class. In the *9–13 Middle School Survey* (1983), they argued that both the more able and the less able were not given enough suitable activities in the majority of schools. And in the most recent *8–12 Middle School Survey* (1985) they similarly argued that overall, the content, level of demand, and pace of work were most often directed towards children of average ability in the class. In many classes, there was insufficient differentiation to cater for the full range of children's capabilities.

This concern about matching appears to be legitimate for our various studies have shown that teachers underestimate their higher attainers, ie the top third of children in their class, and overestimate low attaining children. This pattern of under- and overestimation has now been found across age levels stretching from five year olds through to 15 year olds. In practice this means that high-attaining children are not stretched to their potential, whereas the progress of low attaining children could effectively be blocked by provision of work that is too difficult for them. A common issue to emerge from both British and American work related to this is that teachers very often perceive busy work to be appropriate work.

Assessment

Difficulties also tend to occur in the teacher's assessment or diagnosis of children's work. Our definition of assessment concerns the judgements of right and wrong that teachers tend to make, including ticking and crossing, written comments, and the like. Diagnosis, on the other hand, we define as teacher attempts to acquire a clear view of pupils' misunderstandings and misconceptions through careful questioning. Our consistent finding is that teachers are adept at informal assessment, but they do not diagnose.

It was also apparent that lack of diagnosis tends to be accompanied by a tendency among teachers to limit their assessment to the *products* of children's work. Rarely did they attempt to ascertain the *processes* or strategies deployed by children in coming to their finished product. This is also linked with a stress on procedural aspects of tasks, and mechanical progress through a scheme of work, rather than pupil understanding. As one young pupil intimated to us, it is a case of getting work done and moving on.

David Ausubel (1968) once asserted that if he had to reduce all of educational psychology to just one principle, he would say that the most important single factor influencing learning is what the learner already knows. Ascertain this and teach accordingly. Lack of diagnosis by teachers does, of course, mean that they do not ascertain what children already know, or perhaps more important, what they do not know, and therefore have insufficient knowledge to enable an optimal decision to be made about the next task. It is clear from our studies that this, in no small part, explains the provision of inappropriate tasks to children.

The fruitfulness of this approach in delineating features of classroom teaching which sustain learning experiences of quality (defined in terms of appropriateness) is now acknowledged, and it was on this basis that it was chosen to throw light on the question of concern here – the appropriateness of four year olds' experiences in infant classes.

Method

So how, and in what form was this information collected? This is shown diagramatically in Fig. 3.2.

The teachers were interviewed before the session started to ascertain, in relation to the target children, their description of the activities the children would be undertaking, into which curriculum areas these activities fitted, the reasons why these activities had been chosen, their expectations of what the child would get out of the activity, and whether any problems were anticipated.

The ways in which the activities were presented were then observed and recorded in the classroom. These observations were guided by six questions

1   How is the activity presented?
2   What are the teacher's actual instructions?
3   How clear are they?
4   What is the activity, its supporting materials and adult help?
5   How are children dispersed at points of transitions?
6   Are the activities the same or different from those of the rest of the class?

Having established these, the focus of the observations moved to the child as he/she engaged with the activity. These observations were written up in the form of fieldnotes which recorded the child's response and also the social context in which the activity was undertaken.

Following the completion of the activity an attempt was made to acquire a picture of the child's perception of the activity, and their reaction to it in terms of familiarity, level of difficulty, enjoyment and involvement. An attempt was also made to ascertain their understanding of the activity.

An interview was also held with the teacher at the end of each session in order to gain their assessments of the work completed. The questions which guided these interviews were; Did the child get out of this activity what you expected? Did any of the problems you anticipated arise? Was the activity a success or a failure? Why? In

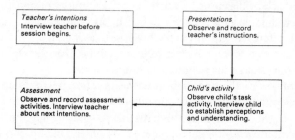

Fig 3.2

the light of this, what will you do next? General comments about the target children and the whole class during that session were also sought.

In addition to the above information, which was acquired in every session, more general information was collected on the school and classroom context. A Class Profile was completed which indicated the class composition in terms of age, sex and whether full time or part time; the basic class organisation, including the morning and afternoon programme; a plan of the classroom incorporating use of space, storage and furniture; contact time with other teachers, and auxiliary, or other adult, provision. A Child Profile was also drawn up including date of birth, age on entry, pre-school experience, siblings etc, and the teacher's assessment of how the child had settled into school, any potential areas of concern and perceived parental attitudes. An actual example of the information collected for one activity is presented below.

Geraldine

Geraldine is 4 years 7 months at the time of observation and is attending her village school. The class has 19 children in it with a two year age range, 4.05 to 6.04. She has received speech therapy outside of school and her mother had warned the teacher that she might be hard to engage in conversation, but the teacher has experienced no such problems.

Teacher intention The teacher indicated that Geraldine would be doing shapes. The reason was to familiarise her with shapes, and to enable her to sort for one property eg colour, shape, size or thickness. The teacher expected Geraldine to develop her ability to visually discriminate between shapes, colours, sizes and thicknesses, and did not anticipate that there would be any problems. This activity was planned for the part-time children only, the full-timers were writing their news, or about Jack and the Beanstalk.

Task presentation When the previous activity had finished the teacher told the group (of part-timers) to sit at the table where the shapes had already been put. The shapes were made of plastic and of various colours, sizes and thickness. Associated cards had been made by the teacher with shapes drawn on them to be used in various ways according to the stage reached. The children were shown what to do by placing some shapes on the card. The teacher's instructions were 'See if you can match all these shapes on the card'. The children appeared to understand and started work immediately.

Task performance Geraldine was working in a group of three children, one boy and two girls. The activity begins at 10.20 am and continues as follows:

10.20 Children are given a large card upon which shapes have been drawn. They have a box of matching shapes (plastic). They have to match the shapes on the card with the plastic shapes (see diagram below):

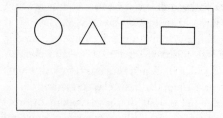

These four shapes are repeated in this sequence on the page. Shapes have to be placed on them.

10.27 Geraldine finishes her matching. Teacher comes over to her and talks about what she has done. (She has them right.)
Teacher then turns the card over. On the back is written – 'What can you fit in here?'
Geraldine is asked to fill the space with as many shapes as she needs.

10.31 Geraldine completes the exercise. She has worked quietly without any interaction with the other two who chat while they are working.
Teacher comes to check Geraldine's work and this time asks her to use thick shapes only (each shape is made with thick or thin plastic).

10.36 Geraldine has finished again.
T. gives her another card and this one has a large triangle on it (see diagram).
T. asks her which shape in the box is the same?
Without hesitation she chooses the triangle.
T. asks her to fill in the shape using the plastic triangles. She starts by putting one at the top and then she fills in the rest as diagram below.

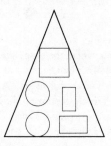

Geraldine's attempt to cover the triangles with triangles!

Teacher returns to group.
T. to G. 'Have you covered your triangles with more triangles?'
G. does not answer.
T. 'Show me a triangle.'

G. Holds one up but still says nothing.

T. 'Are you going to try it again for me?'

G. looks up at T. and smiles.

Her attempt this time (see diagram below).

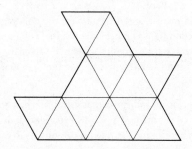

Teacher returns to table.

T. 'Have you used all triangles this time?'

10.40 G. nods.

T. 'Yes you have. Am I going to say it is just what I wanted you to do?'

G. nods.

T. 'Well, not quite. What do you think I might say?'

G. puts her finger in her mouth and says nothing.

T. smiles and puts her hand on G.'s arm. 'Well I'll tell you if you don't know. You have got it nearly right and you have tried hard and been a good girl but do you think you could do it once more and this time don't have any shapes outside the shape on the card?'

G. looks up and takes her finger out of her mouth. She smiles at T. and says 'Yes'.

10.45 G. gets it right. She looks across room at teacher who walks over to her immediately.

T. tells her it is lovely. They exchange smiles.

T. gives her a card with two triangles on it. She asks G. to fill one with small triangles and the other with large ones.

G. achieves this confidently. She has visibly progressed in her familiarity with the shapes.

She goes over to teacher to tell her she has finished.

Teacher returns with G. She praises her correct work.

10.50 T. 'Now I have one more job for you to do. Perhaps the hardest of all. They all have to be put away in the box!

G. looks at T. and they both laugh.

Geraldine carefully fits all the shapes into the appropriate compartments in the box.

It is time to go out to play.

Assessment / Diagnosis

i Pupil interview Focused interviews with four year old children are not easy. In this instance, for example, Geraldine was more interested in talking about her little pony which she got for Christmas than about her shapes activity. Nevertheless it was established that she had found it hard, it was not familiar work, and that she had enjoyed it.

ii Teacher interview The teacher indicated that Geraldine had got out of the activity what she had expected, commenting 'Yes, she experienced difficulties, but I had deliberately wanted to get her thinking and I was careful not to cause her any anxiety'.

She had not anticipated any problems but admitted that Geraldine had problems with the initial use of triangles but that she got it right and had a sense of achievement. The activity was, as far as she was concerned, a success. Geraldine had used shapes with which she was familiar and it had also introduced her to the word triangle, which she didn't previously know, and it gave her the opportunity to sort. In the light of this she would progress Geraldine to sequencing with beads and then pegboards.

The teacher's general comment on Geraldine for that session was that she had worked to the best of her ability and was able to do the work on her own at her own pace most of the time.

Sampling

What has been portrayed above is one 30 minute activity. However in each LEA two children in each of six classes were observed, chosen by the teacher to reflect the range of attainment in her class. Each child was observed for a minimum of three half day sessions during the Spring term, ie approximately 16 hours per class. During this time some 250 activities were observed, an average of over 20 activities per classroom.

Analysis

The analyses of these data centre around various kinds of appropriateness, and these are exemplified below with reference to the example of Geraldine above.

a Appropriateness of activities to teacher intentions. In Geraldine's case the activity presented was appropriate for the stated intention of familiarisation with shapes, sorting, and development of visual discrimination. The activity was also appropriately differentiated, that is, planned specifically for the group of part-time four year olds.

b Appropriateness of presentation. Presentation was appropriate. The group was shown what to do by example, and it was clear to them. Supporting materials were provided.

c Appropriateness of activity to child. The activity was judged appropriate. After some practice on familiar shapes the triangle is introduced and through careful teacher questioning and support understanding is reached. The child's responses in interview support this judgement.

d Appropriateness of classroom organisation. This was judged appropriate.

e Appropriateness of future intentions. The teacher understood that, although appropriate, Geraldine has found it a little difficult. In this light the next planned intention seemed appropriate.

The analysis of each of those questions requires a judgement on the basis of observed data using professional knowledge. But underpinning professional knowledge lie values and ideologies. It was therefore important that the judgements made by the head teachers be subject to checks of reliability and consistency. This was achieved by working in pairs on random samples of activities, and then discussing the basis of any disagreements prior to working on further samples. This continued until inter-judge agreements were extremely high ie in excess of 95 percent. As a further check all the judgements were checked by a third person not involved in the original analyses.

The findings derived from these analyses are presented in Chapter Four.

4 Task Appropriateness of Children's Classroom Activities

The focus here is on the activities undertaken by the children in the classroom and their appropriateness. The structure of the chapter follows the indices of appropriateness outlined in Chapter Three, containing sections on teacher intentions, presentation, matching, task implementation and assessment. In each section the pattern of findings is described, supported by examples from practice. Prior to this however an overview of the organisational and curriculum context of the schools is provided.

Context

The findings are based on the observation of 250 tasks/activities, 22 children and 11 schools.[1] Class size and composition varied greatly. Three classes comprised only four year olds, and ranged in size from 18 to 33; one included only fours and rising fives; three held fours and first years, ranging in size from 16 to 38; another three contained four to six year olds, with a range of 19 to 36, and one held fours to sevens in a small rural school with a class size of 14.

The pattern of groups to which the activities were directed was very similar in each LEA. Approximately 60 percent were carried out in the context of a small group, about one third were class-based activities and the remainder, about five percent, were worked individually. However when working in a group the activities were almost wholly individually based. Very rarely was there a demand for a cooperative group effort. In general the activity pattern was more seated than active,

1 One of the 12 schools had to drop out half way through the study.

in the ratio 3:1, but most, ie 80 percent were associated with some kind of adult presence. Most activities were teacher chosen.

The extent of teacher- to child-chosen activities has been a recurring source of concern in previous literature. Here the pattern of activity choice was considered in each curriculum area using the information provided by the teachers. It was often the claim that activities had cross-curricular intentions and as a consequence more curriculum intentions were started than actual activities. The number of tasks in each curriculum area is presented in Table 4.1 (column N) as well as the proportion of these tasks chosen by the teacher.

Table 4.1 Curriculum priorities and activity choice in each LEA

Curriculum area	LEA A		LEA B	
	% teacher chosen	N	% teacher chosen	N
Spoken language	85.7	56	81.1	37
Written language	100	11	90.9	11
Pre-reading	93.8	32	94.1	17
Story/listening	100	22	100	26
Early number/science	94.2	53	83.8	37
Creative	61.2	31	41.2	17
Play	35.7	14	40	14
PE	100	3	100	8
Music	100	11	100	3
Fine and gross motor skills	73.4	49	89.2	37
Total	83.3	282	81.2	207

This table shows both the curricular priorities of the teachers, and the pattern of activity choice. During the periods of our observations, normally at least six half days through the Spring term, the highest priorities were placed on spoken language activities and early number/science (mainly number) work. High emphasis was also placed on activities which developed motor skills, with pre-reading and story/listening activities coming fourth in their priorities. Intentions for play and for creative work came very low in the pecking order, with only two and six percent respectively of the intentions stated by teachers.

What is abundantly clear from Table 4.1 is that the great majority of activities are chosen by the teachers, and that this is the case in all curriculum areas except play. This pattern held across all classes but was more extreme in some. In one class 46 of the 47 activities observed were teacher chosen, whereas in another only 19 of the 41 activities were chosen by the teacher.

Finally the length of the activities themselves varied widely, from five to 120 minutes. The average length of tasks in each classroom also varied, from 18 to 34 minutes, which may appear somewhat lengthy in view of the concentration span of children of this age.

Teacher intentions

It will be recalled that the model presented in Chapter Three is cyclic, with teacher intentions both starting and completing the cycle. In this section the start of the cycle will be the focus, leaving consideration of the teachers' next planned intentions until later, when it will be seen that teachers were much more successful with the former than the latter.

Teachers were generally able to select activities which were appropriate to their intentions although, as we shall see later, they were not always able to specify them clearly nor, on occasion, to actually implement them. Examples of activities inappropriate to teacher intentions included such tasks as having a child spend 20 minutes colouring in an extremely large circle when the intention was shape recognition, or, in another instance, colouring in when the intention was sorting. Similarly, children spent time tracing round a tree, or round a ladybird, when the intention was learning left to right.

It was not always possible to categorise the link of intention and task as appropriate or inappropriate since teachers often gave multiple intentions, some of which were, and some of which were not, matched. For example the intentions for one child (Sam) were to provide an activity to allow for number language, in this case long/longer, up/down, to do some work on the concept of length, and comparing. The activity designed to achieve these can be judged from the observation log.

11.00   Children have come in from play and are sitting round teacher on carpet. They say the rhyme 'Incey Wincey Spider' and there is a general discussion about the poem. They decide to make a drainpipe from cardboard tubes and spiders from pipe cleaners. Sam's group are going to do this first.

11.05   Sam puts on an apron and starts to paint his tube black. He is finding it difficult to control his brush – and the paint. He is completely absorbed in covering the tube with paint. The paint is thick and there is a fair amount of mess involved! His first tube is covered and he put it to one side. He selects a smaller tube and begins to paint that. He then places both tubes on the window ledge. Auxiliary asks him which tube is longer? He answers correctly. Auxiliary tells him to wash his hands and take off his apron. This he does and looks around to see what to do next.

11.25   Teacher warns children that they have a moment or two before it is time to pack up.

Sam wanders over to the playdough and helps to put it away, he squeezes it between his fingers! He looks totally absorbed.
Teacher calls all the children over to her at the carpet area.

It seems clear from this that some work was done in number language but nothing explicitly on the concept of length, or any comparing. The intention was thus successfully implemented only in part.

In some instances it was not possible to judge whether the intentions had even been partly successful because of the lack of specificity of the intention. For example, 'I hope to use the results of my input on maths and language activities', or 'so that I can work with another group of children'. In another class, the teacher, in a supreme piece of honesty, once stated 'I have very little in the way of intentions today'.

Interestingly, on the odd occasion intentions for children are outside the teacher's control, indeed oppose the teacher's views. In one school, for example, the head teacher had decided that an ancillary would take on the task of providing new children with reading experiences by removing them from the classroom to participate in reading (or trying to read) flashcards. The teacher disapproved of this practice, and not only because it ensured that the children always missed a PE session.

Presentation

All activities have, in some way, to be presented to children – even in free choice situations. The particular concerns here are – did the teachers adequately present their intentions and task demands? Was the presentation clear and understood? Were supporting materials available and appropriate?

In general teachers were reasonably successful in this area, but there was a marked variability across teachers. Like the little girl with the little curl, when teachers were good they were very, very good, and when they were bad they were awful. The difficulties which occurred were in three interrelated areas: where the intentions and task demands were not clear, or were, in some other way, inappropriate; where presentations were inadequately monitored, and where appropriate materials were not available.

One of the concerns about teaching in general, be it primary, secondary or tertiary, is that teachers too rarely indicate the purpose of tasks, instead choosing to emphasise the nature of the activity presented. This type of problem is categorised here as one of inappropriate demand. An example which typifies this hand the intention of 'picture sequencing – to help (the child) think logically and to get the idea of direction'. The activity chosen to fulfil this intention was appropriate, comprising three pictures to be put into temporal sequence. However the activity was presented with the words 'Now we are going to do some colouring in and cutting'.

A very similar example comes from another class. Here the intention was learning about sounds, in particular the sound 'h'. The activity was appropriate to that intention (even though other teachers might not tackle it this way) comprising a photcopied sheet containing hand drawn pictures of a horse, hand, house and hammer together with the single letter 'h'. As above, the instructions concerned not the sound of 'h', or the pictures, but 'colour in the pictures and draw over the letter'. This kind of specification is very likely to affect the child's perception of purpose. In this instance the child, when interviewed, said he had 'coloured things on paper', and had no idea that the letter had anything to do with the picture.

Another example of failure to specify demand was where the teacher intended the child to play with puppets for the purpose of 'enjoying handling the puppets and making up stories about the characters'. However the teacher's instructions consisted of the sentence 'Would you like to play with the puppets?' There was nothing said to the child about why or how the puppets were to be played with, nor any indication that this play would lead to the making up of stories. A very similar scene was played out in another classroom. Here the teacher's intention was to have the child acquire recognition of numbers 1 to 5 through counting, and recognition of numbers of farm animals. Yet the activity was specified by the teacher in terms of 'Would you like to play with the farm?' There was no counting undertaken in the activity and no demand for it.

The presentation of activities in very different terms from the original intention is fairly widespread, as the number of examples indicates. Another difficulty, closely associated with this, is where teachers provide insufficient information for chilen to understand what it is they are supposed to do. In one class for example the children had no idea what was to happen next, simply because they were not told. They were to watch a TV programme on early number but the following extract from the log shows what actually ensued.

11.05   Teacher: 'Line up by the door.'
        They go into classroom opposite for the TV programme with the parallel class. The class sits down behind the other class. One child said 'Are we going to watch TV?' Their class teacher leaves to record another TV programme. The other teacher shows them a vase of violets and some velvet fabrics (both totally unrelated to the programme).

        Programme starts but does not inform children what it is about.

It seems particularly necessary for teachers to ensure that new children, often highly anxious during the first few days, clearly understand what is happening, and is to happen, not only in relation to their own classroom activities but also school-based sessions like Assembly. The following example, fortunately atypical, shows how not to do it.

11 new children came in on Monday – 2 days ago. The teacher tells me they are awful – lots of tears and crying for Mummy – even at five past nine! It is getting her down. The room seems crowded with tables and chairs.

8.55   Children start to come in because it is raining. Usually they have to wait in the playground until the bell goes. The teacher is writing on the blackboard for the older ones, she occasionally comments to a child. One new child cries. The teacher is talking to another parent and takes no notice. The parent helper goes to the child and distracts him with drawing.

9.00   A child goes to the teacher holding up his arms and crying. 'Sit down,' she says, pushing him towards his table. He sits by the helper who reaches for him. Three children are crying now by the parent helper. All need her arms, she tries to touch them all. The teacher shouts at a boy, 'John, that is enough, we'll all cry in a minute'. She tells him off. A boy is dragged into the classroom by the teacher. The teacher and the helper go out leaving three crying, one is holding the helper's hand when she comes back.

9.06   The teacher says sharply 'All line up by the door.' She claps her hands. Two crying children are dragged screaming into the line, one forced to leave his new pencil case on the table.
T. 'Stop that, you're a big boy now.'
Assembly. The infant classes are told they will have to undress after play 'to have apparatus': A new girl cries. Back to class.

9.45   Register.
Teacher: 'After play we're doing apparatus'. A child cries. She's told off. No other explanation about PE.

Here no attempt is made to inform new children that they are to go to Assembly, or what will happen there, and no description or explanation is offered for the prospectively strange practice of taking one's clothes off to 'have apparatus'.

The final form of inadequate presentation occurs fairly frequently in self-chosen play activities where lack of instruction is fairly typical, and where the purpose of such activities often appears unclear to both teacher and taught. This aspect will be taken up in a later section.

A third area of inappropriate presentation concerns the mismatch of the teacher's actual instructions to the activity. In one activity, the purpose of which was to develop the left to right orientation, the teacher gives a demonstration with unpredictable but understandable effects.

10.30   Teacher: 'We're going to do a problem.'
She reminds them about one they did the other day. They are to do a dot to start with, and then start to make the pattern bigger, moving it across the paper. She shows them, drawing a dot on the left of her paper and drawing a

round continuous pattern to the right side of the paper. She chooses another colour and does the same.

The children start to do the same.

Kay, who is sitting at the opposite side of the table to the teacher, puts her dot on the right hand side of the page. From where she is sitting this is the same side as the teacher's dot. She draws from right to left, making the pattern larger as she goes across the paper. She repeats the pattern seven times with different colours. All the other children are doing it the right way.

10.40   The children have to stop because the school nurse comes in to inspect their hair for nits.

Another instance where teacher instructions actually confused children came in a country dancing session. Toward the end of the session the teacher suddenly decided to give instructions different to those on the tape, to the children's evident confusion.

10.25   Tape on again – at the beginning. But the dance they have to do is not the same as the instructions on the tape. Instead the teacher calls out different instructions. So when the tape says dance on the spot, the children have to swing their partners! When the tape says dance around the room, they clap on the spot!

Not surprisingly some children find this extremely confusing.

Another problematic area was teachers' monitoring activity, and the extent to which teachers ascertained whether children had understood the demands. Some did not, or their helper did not, leading to unnecessary confusion. For example one teacher wanted to get them to understand the circle shape and planned and presented an activity which demanded that children use circles to make up a caterpillar. However she failed to ascertain that the children had a concept of caterpillar, and it soon became evident that some did not. Equally typical are situations in which although the teacher offers an acceptable explanation the child does not understand it, or in some cases misses the presentation altogether, because of absence elsewhere in the school. Sometimes such children spent large amounts of time either confused, or off-task, or both, while they waited to gain the attention of the teacher.

Materials

A crucial aspect of adequate presentation is the provision of appropriate materials. Overall this was not a major problem, although inappropriate provision characterised one activity in six. These were disproportionately distributed across classes, however, and it was a problem which affected only a minority of the teachers.

Mandy's experience is typical of the kind of problem in this area. The following extract from the log is self-explanatory.

10.20 As other children arrive back the auxiliary introduced the next part of the activity – a fish game. Mandy has a turn to lower the large magnet into the 'tank' to 'catch' a word which is attached to a small metal ring. She gets the word 'door' which she cannot read. She tries again but has chosen a 'fish' with the metal ring missing so she can't pick it up. The group are getting restless. Mandy points out that she is rapidly running out of 'fish' with rings attached.

Later that same morning Mandy was again frustrated in her attempt to continue her activities when, in a colouring task, she 'tried several coloured felt tipped pens none of which work!'

Meanwhile, in another classroom, Andrew tries to fill in shapes.

11.12 The group are in the Home Corner with auxiliary. They have small lino 'tiles' and are placing them on the floor to make a new surface.

Auxiliary has invited one little girl to try and lay the new floor tiles. Andrew tells her it is wrong.

Auxiliary asks him why.

Andrew: 'They don't fit.'

Auxiliary: 'Why?'

Andrew: 'They are the wrong size. I can still see the other floor.'

He is right. The 'house' floor is an irregular shape but the lino pieces are all rectangular. Therefore the children won't be able to cover the floor properly. The children continue to put the lino pieces on the floor and continue to find the task unsatisfactory.

11.25 Andrew has lost all interest in the proceedings and is sitting gazing across the room at the other children.

Other examples are more straightforward, like providing a shape that can be drawn round.

10.08 T. 'Right, choose a shape you would like to draw round, and tip the others back in the box.' She gives them some paper.

T. 'Have you chosen a shape? Ray, choose a shape.'

He chooses a camel. These are counting shapes not templates. The camel is very difficult to draw round. Ray tries and finds it hard. He has several tries, but manages nothing like a camel. Ray asks the boy if he can have his fish to draw round, but he doesn't get it. Ray's drawing is very unsatisfactory. He turns his paper over and tries again. On the other tables, children are colouring in their shapes. Ray still hasn't managed to draw a recognisable shape yet. The teacher comes. 'How are you getting along with your shapes? Oh, I didn't get you any colours. Sorry.'

10.15 Other children have finished and are sitting by the teacher. Now Ray is trying to draw round the shape with a sticky crayon.

It is apparent that inappropriate or unsatisfactory materials can be linked to increased restlessness or decreased interest. It also appears to be the case that inappropriate classroom management can impact on materials, as in the case of Keith below.

11.20   They are very noisy.
Parent helper takes a girl to teacher – she has had sand put in her hair. Teacher tries to determine identity of culprit! Class continue to be very noisy. Culprit identified by girl – he hotly denies it! Parent helper looks duly shocked.

11.23   Teacher looks harassed. Children restless and noisy waiting on carpet Keith sitting quietly watching.

11.25   Programme starts – (*Playtime* – Radio 4). Teacher can't get sufficient volume. She has to repeat instructions. Teacher: 'Pretend to go paddling.'

11.26   Teacher fiddles with radio and manages to increase volume. Children are lying on carpet. They are much too close together. Told to sit up (programme). They are very noisy and not really listening.
Keith is one of the few trying to listen.
Teacher: 'Children, I am sorry but if you are going to talk I shall have to turn the radio off because you can't hear it.'
Keith has picked up toy cup from the display table and is playing with it.
Teacher asks them to join in the action rhyme. Only a few respond (not Keith).

11.31   Teacher turns radio off because of noise (from children).
(The space is too confined. They cannot carry out the actions without banging into one another.)

In summary, difficulties in both presentation and in materials provision, occurred in approximately one task in six. However this average masks big differences between teachers. Some were particularly impressive in this regard, but some equally unimpressive. There appear to be particular difficulties in four areas – where teachers do not make the real intention or demand clear; where their presentations are inadequate or inaccurate; where presentations are poorly monitored; and where appropriate materials are not provided.

Matching

In contemporary discussions of teaching the term 'matching' entails assigning children work that optimally sustains motivation, confidence and progress in learning (see HMI, 1978, 1983, 1985). As the Plowden Report (1967) argued, teachers must '... avoid the twin pitfalls of demanding too much and expecting too little'. In our previous studies a clear pattern emerged of the overestimation of low attainers and the underestimation of high attainers in the class, findings which provided support to the findings of HMI. In this study it was not possible to choose a sample of children who could easily be categorised high or low attainers, either because teacher did not know the children well enough other than to give a rough estimate (which we used for sampling purposes) or because there were insufficient four year olds in the class to provide any kind of sensible distribution. It is therefore not possible to carry out an analysis on the basis of ability or attainment. Overall, however, the issue of matching is one of the most serious problems we identified since nearly one activity in four was judged to be inappropriate, a pattern which was similar in each class in each LEA. Most of the mismatches in LEA **A** were overestimates, whereas in LEA **B** there was an equal proportion of over and underestimates.

Overestimation

The example presented in Chapter Three was deliberately chosen as a good match. In contrast the following example presents a poor match. The teacher's intention is sorting numbers by colour to provide experience in writing numbers. The activity is drawn from SPMG *Infant Mathematics* Stage 1. The teacher's instructions are 'Now go and get your maths book', and 'do the next page'.

11.30   Mary has taken her workbox from the table and takes out *Infant Mathematics* Stage 1. Sorting. Matching, 1 and 2 (SPMG) Page 10 – write 2. Mary has traced 2 several times, at the top of the page. Under this there are four sets of pictures (see below):

eg

(Mary should put '2' in box)

Mary has written ε beside each set of 2. Auxiliary walks over and asks what she has written. Mary does not reply.

11.38   Auxiliary 'I'll go and get a rubber and rub them out.'
She does so.
Mary does another shape exactly as before, followed by another in the next set below.
Auxiliary counts the pictures with her. Mary counts correctly.
Auxiliary draws 2.

Mary draws.

Auxiliary 'Copy those again.' Rubs out Mary's 2s at top of page.

Mary copies over the shapes. She starts from the bottom in each case.

They end up looking fairly accurate.

Auxiliary. 'Now do the sets where you got them wrong.'

Mary goes back to the picture sets and does them wrong again. (She starts each number from the bottom as she did when tracing the numbers at top of page.) This time she rubs them out herself before the auxiliary sees them.

Mary is nearly crying with frustration. She knows she has them wrong but just cannot get them right.

Auxiliary re-appears from other side of table and tells her not to worry.

11.45   She tries again and gets one right and two wrong. Shrieks with frustration and hits the auxiliary on arm to attract her attention.

Gets two wrong again.

Stands up and covers face with hands shouting 'Oh! Oh!'

Scribbles on second square where she should write '2'.

Auxiliary comes and sits next to her. She smiles sympathetically at Mary and says 'I like that one' – pointing to the only correct one.

Mary shouts to teacher who happens to walk past the table 'I can't do it. It keeps going wrong!' She has tears pouring down her cheeks.

Teacher doesn't appear to really look at her. She says, 'Never mind. it doesn't matter as long as you try'.

She ticks the work and tells Mary she can put her book away now.

This is an interesting case for many reasons. The activity is sensible in terms of the stated intention but the presentation is brief and barren, 'Get on from where you left off yesterday' is all too prevalent an instruction in primary maths work and provides no input or structure to learners. The task is also an overestimate and marked by extremely poor quality interventions from teacher and auxiliary alike – an issue which will be elaborated more generally later. The child's and teacher's later perceptions are also interesting. Mary said that she couldn't do a 2, 'I couldn't do it. It was too hard, I didn't like it. I don't like the books'. The teacher on the other hand rated the activity a success, arguing that she got on with it, and it was a bit of her own work, and concluded 'She seems to like doing her maths book'. When asked what Mary would be doing next in the light of the day's work she replied 'The next page'.

Mary was considered a bright child by her teacher but those judged by their teachers to be below average suffered similarly. Emma was required to carry out some number work from SPMG First Stage *Sorting and Matching*. The page had six sets drawn with one picture provided in each set – a flower, a bird, a snake, a boot, a stick and a lollipop. The demand was for Emma to make a set of 2 by drawing another object in each set.

10.15 Teacher sits by Emma and explains to her that they are going to try and make a set of 2. 'Do you remember we did sets of shoes and drew a ring round them? How many have we got in this set?' Emma says nothing.

T: 'Shall we give it (the flower) a nice yellow centre, and some green leaves and make it look like a daisy?' Emma smiles. T. asks her again how many? Emma says '2'.

T: 'Do you think 2? Just look how many daisies, pointing to it. Are there any more? You draw me one more daisy and we'll see how many daisies are in that set.'

E. starts to draw, teacher starts to help child sitting next to her and E. stops to watch.

10.18 Emma looks in the crayon box. Sits. Puts her hand up and down again. Turns over the page of her book. She fidgets. Looking towards the teacher who has moved away a little.

10.22 Emma draws the simple head of a flower. The teacher comes and talks about the stalk. Emma has a green crayon. Watches the teacher again then faintly draws 2 green leaves. She watches children and teacher again and puts her hand up whenever T. moves in her direction. Teacher comes back 'How many daisies have we got?'

Emma: '2'.

T: 'How many lollipops have we got?' (next set)

Emma doesn't answer. Teacher asked her what flavour lollipop she likes. It was strawberry. T. pretends to lick a lolly.

Teacher: 'Let's pretend this pencil is a lolly, a blue lolly, how many have you got?' Gives Emma the lolly. 'How many lollipops have you got?'

Emma: '1'. Teacher refers back to work on sheet '1' lolly for me. 1 lolly for Emma.' They talk about flavours. Teacher goes.

Emma draws 1 lolly, puts pencil down. In a moment draws lolly a bit bigger. She puts her hand up and stands looking towards teacher.

Emma now alone at table.

10.30 Emma still sitting looking towards teacher. Teacher says 'stop and tidy away'.

Emma clearly did not understand the concepts involved. She did not know how many were in the set. When she was questioned after the activity it became clear that although she could say numbers to three, these numbers did not correspond to reality. She was also asked how many were in the sets she had not completed, and here too she was unable to provide the right answers.

Geraldine suffered a similar overestimation. She had the task of finding out, in the water tray, how many little containers of water it would take to fill a large sweet jar. Geraldine could only count to 5, but it took 22 containers of water to fill the sweet jar. The teacher accepted that Geraldine did not get out of the activity what she expected, and attributed it to the fact that she was unable to be present. Nevertheless the task was rated a success on the grounds that she had a lot of chat with another girl which would have been good for her. She also claimed that she knew Geraldine could not cope with large numbers 'but I wanted her to try the idea'.

In another class Sam was having trouble with his counting. The children had just finished watching a TV programme about counting steps using height and numbers. After the programme the teacher repeated the steps several times with the children joining in the counting. The teacher then said 'We are going to see if we can make steps with our bricks just like they did on the programme. Take some bricks. I don't mind how many, and see if you can make steps without having a gap which you'd have to jump over'.

9.43   Children all trying to make steps. Very absorbed. (Group of 4 children.)
Sam trying very hard to build the staircase.
Teacher all the time using number language as she talks to individuals about their efforts –
'Yours are in twos.'
'Yours are tall steps.'
'You haven't used as many.'
'Yours go up in steps.'
'Sam's making lots of twos.'
Sam has floundered on the step-building. He only achieved making twos. Others are coping with it. Teacher now turns her attention exclusively to Sam.
Teacher: ' Do you want to make another one the same?'
Sam nods.
Teacher: 'Here are three cubes. Can you make a group the same as that?'
Sam gets it wrong.
Teacher: 'Are they the same?'
Sam shakes his head.
Teacher chooses three other bricks and puts them in steps.
Sam takes three others and puts them into same formation.
Teacher: 'That's right, now there are twins, they are both the same aren't they?'
Teacher: 'I am going to leave you all to play with the bricks now.'
Sam immediately leaves group – so do the two girls – leaving one boy still playing with them.

9.55   Sam stands and watches a group who are cutting and sticking pictures from a catalogue.
(Teacher comes to me and says Sam didn't know what the word 'flower' meant last week when they did Mother's Day cards. They had talked about daffodils.)

9.56   Teacher calls Sam over to her. She points to a vase of daffodils and asks what they are. Sam has no idea.
Teacher hands him two daffodils.

Sam puts them in the vase of water.
Teacher: 'Can you see which is the tallest?'
Sam makes no attempt to answer. They have been joined by another boy.
Sam grins at boy.
Boy: 'That one's biggest.'
Sam looks at teacher. She smiles and Sam says, 'That one'.
Boy wanders off looking pleased with himself!
Teacher gives him three bricks, smiles, and says 'Can you make me steps like you did before?'
Sam tries but can't.
Teacher: 'Can I have one brick back now?'
Sam looks quite relaxed but looks at bricks and then at teacher and shakes his head.
Teacher smiles and ruffles his hair, 'Never mind.'
Teacher: 'You play with the bricks for a few minutes and see what you can make.'

In his interview it was clear that Sam lacked the concept of two and did not know how to differentiate red from yellow. The teacher knew he did not know his numbers but nevertheless rated it a success on the grounds that he enjoyed it and experienced numbers.

The examples used so far have been in the area of number, but overestimates occurred in all areas. Emma (a different Emma than the previous example) had a hard time in sewing.

10.20 The parent gives some sewing to Emma. She looks at it as if she doesn't know what to do. A boy next to her pulls the needle out for her but it comes unthreaded and her name comes off too. She tries to work it out, then sits and watches the parent helping another child who is starting his sewing.

10.25 The parent threads Emma's needle. Emma has the needle in her left hand, she puts the needle in the wrong side of the fabric, but in the next hole, she pulls it through, the needle comes off the thread.
Emma tries to fix it, but she can't.
Emma: 'Mrs Green, it's come undone.'
The parent puts it right for her. Emma starts again. She finds the next hole on the right side this time. She does not pull the thread right through so it gets in a muddle. She puts the next stitch in the hole correctly, but the next one is on the wrong side so the thread goes over the edge. She continues to do another two or three stitches until she has to ask for help. The parent untangles it and gives it back without comment. They are sitting on the carpet. The parent is not able to watch Emma because she is helping another child.
An older girl comes and says to the parent: 'Shall I help her?' (Emma)
The parent agrees. The girl takes Emma's sewing and looks at it. She says: 'Oh

look,' and she gives it to the parent who untangles it. The older girl asks if she should watch Emma.

Parent: 'Yes, you can if you like.'

The older girl takes the needle, puts it in the next hole and pulls it through. She goes on doing this with Emma watching until the parent tells her to give it back. Emma carries on and manages to re-thread her needle once. The teacher happened to come at that point and said:

Teacher: 'Oh, Emma can you thread your needle?'

Emma nods. She looked encouraged by this remark. She continues, tries to thread her needle again, but threads only half the wool. The older girl and the parent sort it out again.

And so on....

Not perhaps surprisingly, Emma said later that she found it extremely hard and did not enjoy it.

Sometimes the materials provided actually make the job a good deal harder. Ray was asked to make a Mother's Day card and the teacher showed him a *Mummy* template to enable him to write Mummy inside the card. She did not ascertain if children understood what the word was, or if they understood how to use it. Ray clearly did not, as the following extract shows

9.05   The teacher gives him the *Mummy* template and he starts to do this. Ray and Harry argue about what the template says: 'Daddy ... Mummy'.

Ray insists it says Daddy. They then talk about Mummy and something to do with Readybrek.

They start to tease another boy about his name, making up a new surname. Ray laughs.

Ray starts colouring in again: 'We are working hard'.

He moves the template and colours in the same letter as before. 'y' only, at the bottom of the page. He carries on in the same way starting to write in the template, it moves and he starts somewhere else. His paper has all these disconnected lines on it.

9.55   Ray and Harry creep away, bending double, but they come back when the teacher moves.

Ray: 'Harry, you want to go to the toilet, shall we both go?' (He went just now).

The teacher comes and talks to Harry. He writes his name. She looks at Ray's paper.

Teacher: 'Haven't you done any shapes, Ray?'

She goes and Ray gets another shape – a diamond and draws that more successfully once.

He does more colouring in, using a pencil he draws in the 'y' on the template.

He takes the template, the wrong way up and draws in it, then gets up, goes down the room, comes back, draws a bit. He makes a few round shapes with tails on, then tries the template again doing *mmy* before moving it to the bottom of the page and doing *my* again. Now he is working on the other side of the paper. He stops to talk again. Meanwhile, another boy takes the template and starts doing it carefully. Ray wants the template back, but is able to find one on another table.

In talking to Ray after the task it became clear that the Mummy template represented only a pattern to him, and he was not able to explain anything about Mother's Day. Nevertheless the teacher said that she was quite pleased with his work.

Underestimates

Underestimates of task and child are less easy to characterise. Children simply found the tasks extremely easy since the demands in the activities were those with which they were totally familiar. The examples tend to be mundane. Take Keith for example. The teacher's intention was for matching for number recognition for the purpose of reinforcing knowledge of numbers and colours. The activity comprised a set of assorted toys, and the teacher's instructions, classically, were 'come and sit with me and play with these little toys'.

11.08   Teacher sits at table with children. She asks children to make groups of red toys. Keith does this easily.
Teacher produces a card with circles on and asks him to choose a group which has the same number. He does this. Teacher asks him to look closely at his group of racing cars. After scrutiny he says the shape of one is a bit different. He easily matches all his groups.

It was clear from Keith's actions, and his interview later, that reinforcement of this kind was not necessary for Keith and that he ought to have been doing more advanced work. The teacher thought it a success however, 'he was learning'.

A classic case of underestimation, and of poor differentiation, occurred in the school where two classes were joined together for a TV Maths programme. This programme was repeated every term. Nevertheless all the children watched it every term irrespective of their competence, or the number of times they had seen it previously. In the session observed this was followed by an interesting example of poor continuity. Having watched the TV programme on the concept of 4, there was no follow up. Instead the children did work on the concept of 10! No explanation or demonstration preceded this work and all children did the same thing. The only differentiation appeared to be that the younger children were not expected to get as far in their colouring as the older ones.

This task under-estimated the child being observed (Rodney) and demonstrates only too well the time so often wasted on unnecessary colouring-in activities.

11.23 Sitting all together in front of the teacher. Teacher holds up scrappy pieces of paper with number 10 written on it in pencil. Teacher asks: 'What number is that?' One child didn't know. Rodney had his hand up, was asked, and said '10'. Teacher says, 'Get out your number book and draw me a set of 10 things'. Children go to get books when Teacher calls name.

11.27 Rodney finds his place in his book. Previous page had nine shapes drawn on it and an attempt at colouring them in. Difficult to tell what the shapes are supposed to represent. Rodney goes to get a pencil. A boy puts the pot of pencils on a high shelf where Rodney cannot reach them. Sees me watching and puts them back.
Rodney takes a pencil and starts to draw round a shape. Teacher discovers he has been given the wrong book. Rodney looks at boy next to him. Reaches across and says '10'. Draws round 'tree' shape using a template, which he manages well.
One page now full with 8 shapes. Looks at boy who has gone on to next page, and draws one tree on next page. Counts shapes with pencil – '9'.

11.38 Takes book to Teacher who tells him to colour it in. Watches other children and helps boy to count his shapes. Gets felt tip pen and starts to colour in.

11.55 Has coloured two shapes and is on third. Watches other boys. Does not attempt to colour in, looks at other children colouring.

Tasks of this kind are seen by children to be tedious and often result in poor motivation. In this instance Rodney had little stomach for colouring in another eight shapes and did not do so. Neither did the teacher place any demand on him to complete the work.

In the interview the teacher she said that the tasks had been reasonably successful, and indicated that the next stop would be work on sets of 7!?

The nature of play

So far the appropriateness of classroom activities has been considered across all curriculum areas, but the activities in one area, play, caused more concern than others. Play activities were not a high priority in the classrooms observed and were linked with a high degree of pupil choice.

The lack of opportunities for play can be seen in Table 4.1 where less than six percent of all activities observed fell into this category. Yet it was also the area where most pupil choice was apparent. Over two-thirds of play activities were chosen by the children themselves. It was also the case that some classrooms were almost devoid of play activities, even where good facilities were available. In one class for example the wet area took up one third of the room, but was rarely used. According to the teacher, water play was only used on special occasions, yet the class was a small one, containing 18 'rising fives'. An identical situation pertained in another class in the same authority, although here the size of the class was bigger, 30 children covering the range 'rising fives' to six year olds. Often, it would seem, play was used as a filler activity of unclear purpose.

What then, did play activities look like? Consider the following five short extracts from the logs. All are child-chosen play activities deemed by the teacher to be 'play'.

Keith

10.15 Keith goes to treasure table and picks up the transformer he brought from home. He has a wander then sits on carpet with two other boys who are playing with sticklebricks. Makes no attempt to speak to them but equally looks quite relaxed. Makes no attempt to play with bricks.
Another boy arrives with lego. Keith moves across carpet to join him. Starts to play and begins by taking square base.
Keith: 'I'm going to build a bigger one than you.'
Other boy ignores him.

10.18 Keith starts dismantling 'building', then changes mind and adds some more. Abandons 'model' and returns to sticklebricks. (Leaving half-made lego model on floor.)

10.20 Teacher corrects class and mentions noise level. (They are rather noisy.)

10.25 Keith has made a sticklebrick car.
Keith goes back to the carpet and puts a tall attachment on the car. He shows the boy next to him who looks puzzled but says nothing. Keith puts model on boy's head and starts to move it down the back of child's neck! Boy pushes Keith away.
Keith dismantles his model and starts to throw the pieces at the two boys on the carpet. One pushes him away and the other throws the lego back at him. Keith immediately backs away.

10.30 Teacher tells class to pack away ready for playtime. Keith does so and sits on carpet. Teacher asks him if he helped to pack away. He doesn't answer but rather reluctantly gets up and makes a token gesture of helping another boy to pack up.

Mark

2.09 Mark goes over to a table where four boys have started playing with peg shapes. The tables have parted in the middle and the children are busy dropping the shapes on the floor. An ancillary from the junior class has come in and is hearing a child read at the next table. She is employed for a statemented child in the other class but as teacher is taking a group of juniors for recorders she is 'on loan'. Ancillary is totally ignoring the chaos behind her. The children have started to throw the pegs through the gap again. Ancillary now notices turns round and tells them to stop. They do, but Mark has really entered into this with enthusiasm and promptly starts to 'post' them through again! Ancillary speaks to him sharply telling him to pick them up and stop doing it. He takes no notice.

2.12   Teacher walks across from recorder group and immediately notices pegs. There is an immediate response and pegs are replaced. As teacher passes table again she suggests to children it would be more sensible to play with them on the carpet!

Andrew

11.38   The water tray has bubbly water in it.
Andrew starts to throw the water at boy opposite. Boy retaliates.
Andrew disappears under tray and rummages in cardboard box. He has found a tube. He proceeds to blow through it. The stream of water is not directed at anyone, or anything, in particular, but more a random aim!
Andrew again raids the boxes and finds some large spoons. He fills these with water and throws it with gusto – and with no apparent deliberate aim!
Child disappears into classroom – extremely wet!

11.45   Auxiliary disappears – child has complained.
Auxiliary asks who has made all the mess and Andrew says he has made some of it.
Auxiliary tells group to take off their aprons and go into classroom for a story with teacher.
(In a later observation Andrew is told by the auxiliary that he can choose something to play with.)

11.50   Andrew goes over the large construction set where a boy is building a wall. Andrew knocks down part of a wall. Boy glances at him but doesn't react further. Boy starts to rebuild the demolished part. Andrew sits on the floor watching but does nothing. The boys have not spoken.
Andrew announces to other boy that he is going to knock the wall down again. Boy looks at him and says 'No'. He is beginning to look cross. Andrew looks at him building for a few moments and then slowly stretches out his hand towards the wall. Other boy immediately puts his hand round to try to protect the construction.
They sit looking at each other but don't speak.
Andrew withdraws his hand.

Boy slowly drops his arms. Andrew waits until his hands have dropped completely – and then so does the wall. The demolition is quick, effective, and this time there is nothing left standing.

11.54 Teacher calls to class to pack away their things.

Mandy

10.35 Mandy goes to 'Puppet Theatre' and kneels down on cushions in front of it. She makes a pile of 4 puppets, turns to me holding an empty stick and tells me there is one missing.
 She creates a puppet fight between Billy Blue Hat and Roger Red Hat.

10.45 Suddenly disappears out to play.

11.10 Has come in from play and has gone straight over to the puppets. She has been joined by two other children.
 Mandy becomes the audience – of one.
 Mandy is kicking one of the girls under the table and there is no evidence of puppet play.
 Mandy comes back round the table and tells them they are not doing it right. She starts to play with the curtains.

11.20 Auxiliary calls to her from across room. She asks Mandy to come to her.

These extracts represent fairly typical practice. Several more similar examples could have been provided. They are characterised by such child behaviours as fighting, throwing, knocking, wandering, messing, and ill-considered and half-completed projects. The activities themselves lacked purpose, structure, any kind of clear demand for process or product, or challenge. There was poor monitoring, no discussion, and no extension or assessment. It should be said that some of the children found such activities to be fun, those who were not the victims that is, and the teachers generally felt such activities to have been a success. Any independent appraisal of such activities is likely to be a good deal more sceptical however, and to ponder the role of these in the education of the children.

Part of the problem seems to be a lack of clear teacher expectations for the purpose and performance of such activities. They seem to hold the view that any play is good play. Part of the problem may also be a lack of guidance in the type of choices made by the child. It was certainly the case that many of the activities chosen by the children underestimated them. Whether this was due to a deliberate choosing of familiar and easy work is not possible to say. But teacher-chosen play activities often showed some similar characteristics, as Amy's experience shows.

10.05 Amy is sitting awaiting the teacher.
 Teacher, coming back: 'Oh dear, what have I done, haven't I given you

anything Amy? Come over here and get a puzzle. Would you like to have a try at this one? Do you know what to do, have you done one before?'
(Amy shakes her head. No.)
'Well, you have to take all the pieces out and try to put them in again.' Amy goes back to the table and does the puzzle quickly.
Teacher: 'Amy, I think you could have a go at ... You've done it?'
Teacher talks to other children and helps them.
Teacher: 'Amy would you like to do that one? Pop that back and do this one.'
Amy puts it back in the cupboard. The teacher is changing the children's puzzles fairly often.
Amy is doing a 12 piece puzzle. She is concentrating, looking at the spaces and the pieces that might fit in. She is obviously used to puzzles. She finishes quickly, spins the puzzle on the table and waits, watching the other children.

10.20   The teacher asks Amy about the puzzle she finished.
Amy waits, the teacher calls across to another child.

10.25   The teacher puts the doll's house on the floor for 3 girls. Amy is still waiting. She sits still and watches. She is alone at the table.
The teacher puts a tray on the floor for 2 boys.
Teacher: 'Amy, bring your puzzle please this way, it's very good. What would you like to do?'
Amy looks at the cupboard but doesn't say anything. The teacher finds a puzzle.
Teacher: 'Do you think you could do that?'
Amy nods, takes it eagerly and goes back to the table. She takes the pieces out, puts the four corner pieces in the right place. (It's a 15 piece puzzle.) She again looks busily at the pieces, obviously very capable (a Paddington puzzle).

10.30   She finishes it, picks it up and puts it in the box, fitting together, complete. She puts the lid on and looks towards the teacher who is busy with all the others on the floor. Amy waits, Teacher is busy, then
Teacher: 'What have you made?'
Amy answers the teacher's questions: 'Paddington Bear ... he's making something ... stirring it up ... spoon ... d'know ... Mummy.'
Amy doesn't offer anything, she just answers the teacher's questions. The teacher asks her to put it away, then teacher has to go to help others in the toilets.
Amy puts it away and sits in her chair at the table.
Amy waits and watches the children playing on the floor.

The puzzles chosen clearly underestimated Amy although the teacher did at least monitor Amy's performance and attempted, albeit with some difficulty, to draw out her understanding of what she had achieved.

Having commented adversely on the majority of play activities observed it should be said that they can be, and indeed are, successful, and in order to balance the picture two examples are presented which led to rich interaction between children in child-chosen activities.

1.55 Karen is playing with the houses and people from *The Village with Three Corners.*
Karen: 'I have got to go and do the shopping.'
Other girl: 'Wait for me, I'll come with you and do some too.'
Karen: 'No because I've got to go out somewhere else to have a party with Mrs Redhat.'

2.00 Takes Mrs Redhat out of the house.
Boy: 'The daddy isn't allowed in and Roger is watching while he bangs and knocks on the door.'
Karen: 'Why can't he come in?'
Boy: 'Coz he's come home late again.'
Karen looks puzzled while boy continues to bang on the door and call to Roger to let him in.

2.05 There is a sudden interruption at the other side of the classroom. The parent-helper who is frequently with this class has arrived dressed up as a frog. She is wearing a frog mask and the rest of her is covered with green Marks and Spencer's plastic bags.
Children all run over to see her. (Teacher did not know this was to happen and there is great merriment.)

2.08 Children all go back to their playing after having joined in the fun. There is animated conversation and imaginative play in Karen's group –
'Mrs Redhat said I've got to guard the house while she's out.'
'Mrs Bluehat has gone away as well.'
'The witch is following them.'
Rip has just had an accident! He has 'flown' through the air and has apparently sustained a broken leg! He is now ensconced with Roger who is ill in bed!
'Come upstairs with me.'
'Mrs Redhat has just come home she has broken her leg, too.'
'How did that happen?'
'She banged it on the house.'

2.15 Boy arrives with some animals from the toy farm: 'Look, the ducks are going into Mrs Bluehat's house.'
Teacher arrives and hears the latest event! Teacher: 'Oh, dear, Mrs Bluehat won't like that because she doesn't like animals.'
Boy to teacher: 'Mrs Redhat has broken her leg and she hasn't got enough money to get it mended.'
Teacher: 'Perhaps the other people in the village will feel sorry for her and collect some money so that she can be made better.'

2.25   Karen rushes over to the maths area and comes back with a handful of cardboard money.

2.25   Teacher: 'Oh good, now she'll be all right.'

In the next excerpt another Karen, in a different class, is playing with multi-link cubes, which brings forth much number language as well as enjoyment.

10.55   The children are coming in after play and sitting down with their books, or toys. The teacher tells the group who were playing with the toys to go and do their work on their library books.
Karen, playing on the floor, helps the parent to put away a box of toys.
Helper to Karen: 'While I'm playing with Tony, you play with Laura. I can't play with two at the same time.'
Karen plays with the multi-link cubes, fitting them together.

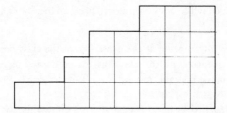

11.05   The teacher asks another group to sit down and do their work. Karen, however, can carry on. She starts playing with the unifix. She fits the cubes together in a long line. She holds it up, smiling, 'Who . . .'. It breaks and she tries to jam it in the box. She stops to listen to the helper who is talking to nearby children about tidying up.
Karen holds her two pieces together to make a bridge for Neil to drive his motor cycle through.
Karen's pieces are the same length.
Karen: 'I've made walky legs. They are the same.
I wanted them to be the same.'

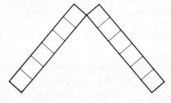

Karen walks around with the pieces now joined together, then goes to the box with a girl and takes some more pieces.

Karen: 'There's two more there.'

Girl: 'People I don't like I'm going to send on holiday. I'm going to send R on holiday. She's the one on your table I don't like.'

Karen does not respond. She fits cubes on her two rods, first on one, then the other, keeping them the same length.

Karen: 'They're the same. Yes they're the trousers.'

Karen: 'And it's getting bigger – look at those, they're getting more and more bigger ... watch out, watch out. Mine is getting taller than yours.'

Karen: 'Let go of it, I'll hold it.'

She grabs the girl's rod, but doesn't hold it and the girl's long rod falls and breaks.

Karen: 'Molly, polly it's a ————?'

G: 'Mine is the biggest'.

Karen: 'Look at this. Mine is getting more and more bigger' (laughs)

The other girl has some pegs now.

G: 'I've got lots of sweeties, you've only got one sweetie.'

Karen takes no notice. Then she looks in the empty box.

Karen: 'Oh, you've got all the mostest. Look at mine.'

She holds her two long rods up. She 'walks' them across the carpet. One breaks, she has to mend it twice. She takes it to the helper.

Karen: 'Look, Mr P.'

Me: 'How did you make them exactly the same?'

Karen: 'I started off with 1-1, 2-2, 3-3, then right up to the top.'

(She points to each leg in turn as she speaks)

Karen takes the rods to the teacher.

T: 'Tell me about these, then.'

Karen: 'They're the legs.'

T: 'Why are they the same height, you matched them up did you? Can you tell me about the blocks, are there more in one than the other?'

Karen tells her something I can't hear.

Karen puts the blocks away.

Play activities can be successful as high quality learning experiences, but they tend not to be. This is not a criticism of play *per se* but of what typically passes for play in the classroom. Our judgement is that the most successful play activities observed were where there was some kind of adult presence and structured discussions during the proceedings. The role of the teacher and the auxiliary in those and other activities is taken up in the next section on task implementation.

In summary, one task in every four was mismatched in this study with slightly more overestimates than underestimates. The quality of matching varied greatly from teacher to teacher. The mismatches appeared in every area of the curriculum and were worst in child-chosen play activities. The play activities observed gave cause for concern, many lacking any apparent purpose or demand, and supported by little adult presence and discussion. In several classrooms play activities simply took on the role of filler.

Task implementation

It might be thought that if the teacher's intention and presentation were both appropriate, and the activity was matched, then a satisfactory learning experience for the child was guaranteed. Unfortunately this is not so. Indeed one of the concerns which became evident in the analyses of the observations related to the number of times good planning and good activities came to nought because of the teacher's, and/or auxiliary's, inability to implement the activity effectively. The factors which appear to be responsible for this are considered under two general headings – classroom management and task management.

Classroom management

Poor classroom organisation showed itself in many forms – lack of pupil involvement, wandering about, interruptions, lack of interest or motivation and poor use of resources. At the level of the individual child this poor organisation can lead to distraction and poor attention to the task in hand. Yet this attention or involvement is critical because it is a necessary condition for learning – no attention, no learning. Yet often children messed about, as we saw in the examples of play activity, with seemingly little teacher or auxiliary awareness. Indeed the observers reported concern at such lack of awareness in over one third of the tasks observed.

Lack of involvement was not only apparent in play activities, as Geraldine's efforts at writing her news illustrates.

> 9.50 Geraldine takes her book to check which page to draw on.
> Teacher shows her and says that Geraldine knows what to do. Geraldine agrees. Geraldine sits down and starts picture. Works quite quickly making a pencil drawing – she adds some dark green colouring in.
> Geraldine's group is having a pencil sharpening session! Their coloured pencils are breaking as fast as they try to use them. However, their pencil-sharpening techniques are improving!
> James notices that Geraldine is wearing a new skirt and tells her he likes it. She looks very pleased and smiles at him.
> Natalie and Geraldine now embark upon a black pencil comparison conversation! They decide they are all as black as each other.
> Natalie and James have a 'silly conversation'. Geraldine says nothing but giggles with them.
> Natalie: 'I feel silly today.'

James: 'You're not as silly as an ice-cream running down the street!'
This is greeted by fits of laughter from the three children.
Geraldine sharpens yet another pencil.

10.15 Geraldine is now busily colouring in her picture.
She is now sharpening her pencil again. There is now quite a deliberate pencil-breaking session being executed by Geraldine. She is pressing too hard – and knows it!
Geraldine sharpens yet another pencil.

10.25 Natalie moves the bin away – into which the pencils are being sharpened.
Natalie has obviously become irritated by Geraldine's constant sharpening presence!
Teacher calls across to Geraldine: 'There will be no pencil left in a moment. Please bring it to me, and your picture.'

The pencil breaking and sharpening routine is clearly learned at an early age, and in this example was a good game for over half an hour.

Wandering off is also typical. Andrew was supposed to be making a model with playdough. He works for ten minutes before wandering off. He is brought back, makes desultory attempts to continue the activity but then wanders off again.

10.28 Andrew now wanders off to the corner of room and puts on a glove puppet. He then plays with a toy car.
Auxiliary calls across to him: 'That car belongs to Robert, Andrew, so you must put it back.'
Andrew puts it down and wanders off again.
He finds some cardboard box models of houses and bangs them up and down on the table. Another boy goes over to him and tells him to stop. He does.
He returns to the table and picks up the board again. He wanders across to teacher with the board.
Teacher tells him to take the board back to the table. He does.
He wanders round room again and finds a pile of tracing paper. He handles it thoughtfully for a moment and then runs off.
Auxiliary calls him. She wants him to make sure he has his 'model' on his board. He hasn't! He doesn't look remotely interested anyway.
Auxiliary persuades him to make another model if he can't find his so that he has got one.
He starts to make a very 'scrappy' model. He uses the head from another child's model. Child protests and auxiliary tells Andrew to give it back.
He puts lumps together with no apparent form and then destroys his name! He wanders off again, stands idly handling a toy from the worktop, and gazes round room.

10.40 Teacher tells all children to pack away and get out 'tuck'.

There was a tendency for such wandering to occur more often in free choice settings. The following short extracts record the same girl's wandering activities three weeks apart.

Children are given a warning about their behaviour – no thumping – some boys are rather unsettled today. The teacher asks them to tidy up before playing, and those who were doing patterns are to go to her and finish them and show her. The last group are to wait for their turn to do patterns.

Kay takes no notice of these instructions but moves about the room visiting briefly the home corner, the shop, where she touches a packet and picks up an egg box, the home corner again, the book corner, the shop and then settles at the drawing table.

(and three weeks later)

She wanders looking for her friend who is still doing chicks. Kay goes to her, then beckons her to come to the drawing table. Kay wanders back in the other room, looks at sand and paints. She sees her friend washing her hands, goes and talks to her, waiting for her. Then Kay heads to the door of the cloakroom where they played before, but her friend doesn't follow.

Kay goes to the puzzle corner, looks, then goes to home corner, looks, watches, then she goes to the puzzle corner, looks around, then goes back to home corner and sits at the table.

Wandering activity in free choice situations was exacerbated in one class where play sessions appeared inappropriately lengthy. Sessions of 45 minutes were common and sometimes lasted nearly an hour.

Previous studies on pupil involvement have argued that it is created or sustained by teacher behaviours such as poor general awareness, lack of adequate mobility and supervision, a set of teacher competencies which could be covered by the more general term of monitoring. In addition to monitoring however is the ability to control noise and movement. An example was given earlier where a radio programme was abandoned because of the noise level and this was not an isolated occurrence, although it was more apparent in certain classes. The auxiliary in one class had to abandon a reading session because of the noise as the following extract shows.

11.50 Auxiliary then starts to read from same supplementary reader used earlier by teacher – about horses.
Auxiliary asks group where she should begin reading.
They tell her – with mixed success.
She starts to read. (The noise is so great that I cannot hear her although I am positioned very close to group.)

11.55 Auxiliary tells children to go and get something to play with because it is too noisy for them to hear her.

Just as children are about to go teacher arrives and asks to see their houses. Group collect them from worktop at side of room. Teacher has a perfunctory glance and moves away without commenting. Teacher and auxiliary do not communicate in any way.

Teacher shouts to class to get their coats on ready to go home or to go to dinner. Dinner lady appears and 'helps vocally with this exercise'!

12.00 Children leave room.

The final aspect of classroom management considered here is the optimal use of resources. Teachers often work in less than ideal conditions, as the findings in Chapter Two indicate. It is all the more necessary, therefore, that the resources available, be they space, equipment or facilities, be used to best advantage. This did not always happen, but rather than present examplars, one observer's evaluative comments on two of her day's observations in the same class makes the point succinctly.

The teacher had a sensitive and appropriate approach to the children which reassured them during the session.

The class was poorly equipped. There was only one small cupboard of maths and pre-reading equipment which had already been well used. This may explain why the teacher resorted this morning to the use of stationery materials to vary the activities.

The only other equipment there was the water container which the teacher did not use. There were two large blackboards which were stored in the room, these were not used either. This lack of equipment may account for the class organisation, where the children did the same activities at the same time. This restricted the teacher's opportunities for individual teacher/child contact.

The teacher had a caring, sensitive attitude: she presented the work in an appropriate way, it was unfortunate that the work itself was not all appropriate for this child.

The teacher had no help today, she normally did have some help, a parent or ancillary sometimes. She had a fairly small class of 16 children so the teacher/child ratio was better than many places.

All the children were doing table based activities for the whole session except for the four at the end sticking a class model. This was a waste of opportunity for the children and of space and resources. Half the room was hardly used – the area with the water play and painting table. The water tray was empty and I understand it was rarely used. There was little time to use the home corner – mainly just before or after playtime rather than a planned time to play.

Task management

If we narrow our focus from the way the class is managed, to the way the tasks or activities are managed, a different but associated set of issues appears. Four of these are considered below. These are: poor implementation due to lack of demand; lack of necessary input; interruptions; inappropriate inputs.

It often seemed that whatever the child produced was deemed acceptable, and in many cases the child completed the work in very short time and with no thought or care after having been off task for much of the time. The following example has been chosen since it links a high degree of non-involvement, followed by a very poor attempt at the task, which was nevertheless accepted by the teacher as a success. The activity demanded the making of a robot either using shapes, construction or painting.

9.50   Keith arrives at Lego table.

     He selects several pieces of Lego and starts to construct a platform arrangement. He is singing to himself whilst doing so and is obviously very absorbed.

9.55   Keith has left group and is now fighting two other boys in the corner. The target appears to be the toy dog 'Spot'. Joe wins and clutches Spot. Keith looks on uncertain as to what to do. Teacher intervenes. Keith then starts to play with large construction toys nearby. He is now arranging and re-arranging bricks on his own. (Only one girl is left in the Lego group.) He is making no attempt to make a robot. He is making a space in the large building bricks box into which he can put a small Lego man.

10.00   He places man in bricks and wanders over to a boy and girl nearby. He impresses girl by standing on one leg and putting foot on head. (This also impresses me!)

     Girl goes across and takes Lego man from hiding place. Keith wanders over to retrieve it.

     He and another boy make another space and he is very firmly holding the man. He hides the Lego man in a corner behind several layers of bricks.

10.05   Keith and the other boy are still playing with the large bricks – hiding the Lego man in different places.

     He looks aggressively at a third boy who has joined the group. He pokes boy who looks cross and stands his ground.

     Third boy knocks down bricks and Keith hits him.

10.10   Teacher calls Keith to her. She suggests he draws a picture of a robot.

     He takes a pencil and proceeds to complete the drawing rapidly and colours it blue.

In another LEA Rodney was enacting a similar scene in response to the ubiquitous demand to draw a picture and write a story. He spent nearly an hour drawing a picture very rapidly, then scribbling over it, fighting another boy, scribbling again to the extent that the picture was totally obscured. The observer wrote, 'The target child had little attention from the teacher. The creative writing session took one hour altogether. The child ended up with exactly the same sentence he had suggested at the beginning. Most of the time he spent drawing was a boring waste of time. He copied the writing quickly and easily in the last minute or two.'

A second difficulty affecting task implementation was where an input to the child was required which was not forthcoming. An example of this was a maths activity, part of the school maths scheme, which comprised a tray containing dry sand, various containers and a commercially made stand with a trough at the top and wheel underneath. By pouring sand into the trough the wheel is turned. The purpose is to assess mathematical language, and as such the auxiliary was present to ascertain children's language and understandings and to record them. What actually happened was as follows:

11.17   Ken arrives at sand. Puts dry sand into trough to move wheel. Uses spade to fill trough, then selects bottle to fill and pours that into trough.
Decides to fill toy submarine with sand and then reverts to playing with wheel.
Ken selects a bucket and takes it to sand tray.
Auxiliary asks, 'What is happening here?'
Ken now puts bucket at base of wheel to catch the sand as it drops.
The other boy then takes an interest and he pours sand in the top while Ken collects it in the bucket at the bottom.

11.25   Teacher tells children to pack up their things and come over to her when they are ready.
Ken does not respond. Most of the other children don't either!

This would appear to be a very poor attempt to ascertain Ken's conceptions to the detriment of his development and her records. It may be rightly claimed that this is a skill which one would not expect an auxiliary to have, but if so the auxiliary should not have been involved.

An experience that Ryan had was not satisfactory for a similar reason. The purpose of the activity was colour recognition through painting. Available were six pots of mixed powder paint, newspapers, a large piece of white paper to paint on and a parent helper (p/h).

2.00   Ryan has decided to paint. Teacher helps him with his apron.
Paints are already mixed and there is newspaper on the table to protect it.

2.01   Ryan takes a large sheet of white paper. He paints a yellow 'sun' in the sky and a long yellow strip at the bottom of the paper.
P/h asks him what he is painting and what colour he is using. No reply. Paints blue over the yellow strip.
Has made no attempt to converse with his peers, but very watchful of other children's activities. Ryan has added black to his picture.

2.10   He now selects white paint. It is very thick. He laughs and says to the p/h that it looks a bit like jelly.
He is happily absorbed in his painting and although aware of the other children they don't distract him.
He now adds red paint very liberally. He volunteers that this is a fire.
P/h says this would make it nice and warm.
A child who has just joined the group wants the black paint. P/h looks at one of the pots near Ryan and asks Ryan if it is the black? (It is brown.) Ryan 'No, it's blue'.
Ryan adds some more yellow to his picture. P/h who is engaged in conversation with child next to her suddenly turns to Ryan and asks him the name of the colour he is using. He can't tell her.
The yellow pot has been moved to the other side of the table by one of the other children. Ryan is determined to get some yellow and leans perilously across the table and manages to bet a brushful.

2.20   Another p/h comes over to table. She looks at Ryan's painting and asks him if he would like to come over to her and make a 'junk' model. He takes no notice of her and continues with his painting. Paper now almost completely covered with yellow and red.

2.28   Ryan still painting, the paper is now saturated with paint – still mainly yellow and red.

P/h asks him which colour he is using at the moment. He says white (it is yellow).
He suddenly stops painting and goes to sink to wash his hands.

Here we see three clear indications that Ryan did not know his colours yet no attempt was made to teach him these. As such a golden opportunity was lost, and a good intention subverted. Also notice that the child is not informed of the purpose of the activity, only that he can choose to paint. Whether the parent helper knew the purpose is unclear. Inevitably therefore the child's view of the activity was that he had done a painting.

A third area of difficulty of implementation is a common one particularly in the infant school, and concerns interruptions. In our previous study of infant children (Bennett et al, 1984) teachers attempting to hear children read often allowed themselves to be harassed by other children in the class. This leads to the teacher's attention being removed from the reader, and often to distraction and/or loss of interest in the reader. This phenomenon was also observed in this study. One example will suffice.

1.48   Teacher asks Caroline to get her reading book and sit with her.

1.52   Reads one page to the teacher, who is interrupted by a message brought by two children from another class.
T. writes reply.
Caroline reads three pages. Teacher tells off child by the sand. T. talks to a girl about writing letters. Caroline read two more pages. T. admires two children's writing. Caroline reads two more pages. T. tells off two children and directs another to an activity. Tells off child still dressing (after PE). There is a queue by the teacher. Caroline is now reading pages 14 and 15.

2.08   Teacher says she can have a new book.

In our previous studies we have complained about this practice of dual queueing ie hearing a child read at one side of the desk whilst reacting to a queue of children at the other. We criticised such practice for being fair neither to the child nor the teacher, and that view still prevails. It is a prime example of poor management.

The fourth and final area of difficulty of implementation is characterised by activities where children ought to be making personal inputs but are prevented from doing so, usually by auxiliaries in this study. A typical example of this was a cooking activity with a group where children were each to make a biscuit in the shape of a house. The curriculum area into which the teacher categorised this was science, since it involved weighing, colour recognition and heat. What actually took place, however, was that the auxiliary did all the weighing and cooking. The only activity that children were involved in was stirring a bowl.

A more extreme experience happened to Keith, who was to paint a bear.

9.45 Keith arrives at paint table having donned apron en route. On table is a selection of coloured tissue paper, mixed powder paint (six colours), glue, crayons, large pieces of computer paper and large sheets grey sugar paper.
Parent helper draws faint pencil outline of 'Daddy Bear' on sugar paper.

9.55 (PE and playtime intervene.)

11.05 The brown paint has been mixed. Keith starts to paint. Parent helper comes over to him, takes the brush from him and shows him how to outline the ear. Proceeds to complete ear! Starts second ear, outlines it and then tells Keith to fill it in. Then tells him to paint head.
Keith has painted an arm and then another arm below it, while parent helper's attention was momentarily diverted!

11.15 Keith has finished his painting. Parent helper tells him to wait. He does. Parent helper gives him a brush with blue paint on it. She asks him to do an eye – and then the other eye. She then does the mouth!
Keith takes off his apron. Parent helper tells him they haven't finished yet.

11.20 Teacher: 'Stop what you are doing. Let me see your face then I'll know you are listening.'
Teacher: 'Now come and sit on the carpet.' Children make their way to the carpet.
(Parent helper appears and takes Keith's picture to teacher – parent helper has painted short trousers and a tie on the bear. Also the 'spare' arm has disappeared, the bears have been cut out and mounted on a sheet of sugar paper. Teacher says she is delighted with it.)

It is not clear here whether the teacher was delighted with Keith or the parent helper!

There is a deal of implied criticism of the quality of ancillary/helper intervention strategies in the above examples. Much concern was expressed in observer judgements concerning the nature and appropriateness of intervention from teacher and auxiliary alike, sometimes exacerbated by what was seen as poor teacher-auxiliary communications. The lack, or lack of clarity, of teacher expectations of auxiliaries, and lack of adequate monitoring of auxiliary actions by teachers was evident. In some classrooms, at least, the teacher appeared to implicitly consider the auxiliary as a surrogate teacher and to accord her autonomy as a consequence. But it was in such situations where task management suffered the most.

Much the best use of auxiliaries was where the teacher knew what she wanted and made that clear. The observer made the following evaluative comment of a teacher who was excellent in this respect.

> The teacher had organised the class so that she could work closely with small groups (4 or 5) on the 'length' work; other groups were having close contacts with adults too. The parent and assistant had been given instructions on what to do, including the language and concepts that the teacher wanted the children to experience.
>
> Everything worked smoothly. There were no problems. The teacher was not constantly bothered by children. She had time to talk to children who did come to her – their conversation was of value to the children's work and was rarely related to management. This child/teacher interaction was of high quality, and encouraged the children to progress and produce high standard of work.
>
> The teacher must have spent hours preparing her work, that of the two adults and the children. It was all well thought out from a curriculum point of view. She says she does this every day – indeed there is a photocopied daily timetable which has to be planned every day. Work was followed through from day to day – with a reinforcement of the last work.

That the teacher instructions were faithfully followed can be seen from the extract below.

9.05 Register, then Assembly.
During assembly, the parent looks at the instructions the teacher has left for her. She is to do cookery. She has the recipe, the preparation and what to talk about whilst they are mixing – the names of ingredients, smells, powders, describing the mixture, sticky syrup, etc. Since last week the teacher has made a large, very strong cooker out of cardboard boxes, and a sink unit with a bowl and taps. There is a table covered with a brightly coloured tablecloth; a pram; a pushchair; a container for dolls, no beds, but a long rail of dressing up clothes.

9.40 The parent helper talks to the group and asks them about Mother's Day which is on Sunday. She mentions: chocolate oat sweets, sultanas, margarine, syrup, chocolate, oats.
Emma puts her hand up and nods when the parent talks about having porridge for breakfast.
Emma: 'It's a bit sticky, isn't it?'

She looks pleased to do it.

The parent puts margarine in each bowl. She asked one boy how many spoonfuls are needed – Emma smiles when they start to put the syrup out.

She puts some chocolate in.

Parent: 'Do you help Mummy?'

Emma nods.

Parent: 'It's very sticky.'

Emma puts some syrup in the bowl, she holds the syrup spoon and watches the syrup fall off.

Emma: 'It's like ice now isn't it?'

The parent takes Emma's spoon and gets the rest of the syrup off it.

Emma stirs the mixture.

Parent: 'Do you think it is going to taste nice?'

Child: 'I do.'

Emma: 'Me too ... it's stiff.'

A boy: 'You just wait till we taste it. Yum, yum.'

This teacher based her whole organisation around the presence of an auxiliary or parent helper and the quality of the children's experience was, as a consequence, improved.

Finally, lest it be thought that most, or the majority, of auxiliary actions were inappropriate, which they were not, another example of what was perceived to be appropriate auxiliary input in cooking playdough is presented below.

2.00   Children are round a table with the auxiliary.

Auxiliary: 'I noticed the other day that our playdough is looking a bit hard. In this bag I have brought the ingredients we need to use to make some more.' She takes them out of the bag one by one and asks the group to name them as she does so. All children very engrossed. Then explains they have to have the right quantities to make it. Tells them they can all have a turn to measure an ingredient.

Karen has her turn and successfully measures half a cup of salt.

Children have all had a turn to put the ingredients into a pan.

Auxiliary: 'Next we need a cup of cold water. How do we know which is the cold water tap?'

2.05   Auxiliary and group go across to the sink. Karen is the first to arrive and correctly identifies the tap. Water is measured and the group return to the table. Karen continues to be totally absorbed (as do the other children).

Mathematical language being used constantly – full, half, nearly full, not quite enough, etc.

Auxiliary: 'Now we put in cream of tartar'.

Karen: 'Queen of Hearts made some tarts' – Greeted with appreciative giggles from the group.

Constant reinforcement of the names of ingredients, what is happening and participation encouraged – and received.

2.10   Children now all have a turn to stir the mixture. One boy says it sounds like muesli when he stirs it.

Children asked to choose a food dye. (Options red or blue.) Four want red, one wants blue.

Auxiliary: 'Well what shall we do? If we mix the colours we'll get purple.'

Karen: 'Lots of us want red. Only Gary wants blue.'

General agreement and Gary acquiesces.

Dye is added to mixture. Gary claims it is pink not red! Discussion as to why it is pink.

Auxiliary: 'Now we are ready to cook it. Let's go to the cooker but remember it's very hot so stand back.'

Children stand round cooker while auxiliary stirs the ingredients. Lots of chatting about cooking at home etc. Also auxiliary mentions the pancakes which they made at school last week.

Children begin to get a bit restless. They cannot see in the pan while it is on the cooker. Auxiliary has taken it off to show them what is happening several times but obviously needs to cook it.

Auxiliary: 'You can go and sit down now if you want to. This is nearly ready and I'll bring it over to you in a few minutes.'

Karen is the first to sit back at the table. She chats to a girl next to her.

Karen: 'I'm going to make a pasty with the dough when it's ready.'

Girl: 'So am I.'

Auxiliary arrives back at the table. All now very interested again as the contents can be seen.

Auxiliary: 'The pan is still very hot.'

2.20   Auxiliary starts to take the dough from the pan. She gives each child a lump of warm dough. Lots of general comment – 'It feels brill!' 'It's really smooth' (Karen). 'It's very soft.' 'Nearly cold now.' 'Can't smell it.' 'It's pink.' 'Nearly red.'

Karen now starts to make a pasty. Asks for rolling pin.

Auxiliary: 'You know where to get it.' This promotes spate of collecting cooking equipment (various shaped cutters being top of the list).

2.25   Auxiliary: 'You can play with the dough now and I'm going to get another group and make some more. I wonder if they will choose blue?' Gary immediately agrees that they will!

In summary, task implementation has been considered in terms of two inter-related aspects of class organisation, classroom management and task management. Poor implementation which shows itself in a lack of pupil involvement, wandering about and other behavioural distractions, was seen to be related to poor teacher monitoring, and was exacerbated when juxtaposed with poor control of noise and movement, and use of resources.

Four issues were discussed under task management; poor implementation due to a lack of demand; lack of necessary inputs; interruptions; and inappropriate inputs. Concern was also expressed at the frequency of the poor management of auxiliary and other assistance, particularly in terms of lack of clarity of expectations and insufficient monitoring of auxiliary activities. We are only too well aware of the demands on teacher's time in the classroom, but an improvement in the use of auxiliaries could, as we have tried to show, have far-reaching implications for the quality of classroom life of both teachers and children.

Task assessment/diagnosis

Several references have already been made to the concern about lack of teacher/auxiliary awareness and monitoring, and to teachers judging activities to have been a success even when palpably they were not. Examples have also been quoted of teachers confusing children by praising incorrect work, using criteria other than correctness despite task intentions to the contrary, auxiliaries or parent helpers failing to identify children's understandings, or, having identified them, failing to do anything on that basis. These examples are not atypical. Teachers and other adults did not diagnose the children's understandings of what they were doing, indeed rarely seemed to assess anything at all in any formal sense.

When children's work was assessed the remarks tended to be perfunctory – 'good', 'great', etc, but children were rarely questioned about the substance or quality of their work, or given suggestions for extension. The following extract is presented simply because it represents a rare occurrence, where the teacher was not prepared to accept the first thing that a child produced.

1.20   Everyone begins to play. Wendy is by the paint area, three others already have aprons on. The teacher comes to see if they have enough brushes.
T: 'Help yourself to paper, you can start as soon as you're ready.
Wendy puts an apron on by herself.
T: 'Well done, good girl.'

1.25   Wendy starts painting. The teacher comes and moves them over to make room for another girl. Wendy is painting without looking at the others, or talking. She goes to the teacher – who looks at her house painting.
T: 'What about your garden?'
Wendy tells what is in her garden.
T: 'What about the front? You've got some grass, haven't you?'
Wendy has painted a house with a roof and six windows, some grass and a garden path. She used several colours.
She finishes and goes to the teacher.

Lack of assessment and diagnosis of children's understandings is worrying because without it there cannot be any clear idea of children's progression or development. And without a clear view of where children are, there can be no clear view of where they ought to go next ie the teacher's next intention.

The evidence indicates that this indeed was the case. One fifth of all the teacher's statements of what activities they would be giving the child next were judged inappropriate, and, as usual, there was marked variability across teachers, some being very successful, others a good deal less so. A classic example of the latter is that of Mary, quoted earlier, who breaks down in frustration at her inability to complete her number work. The teacher, completely failing to monitor this, states that she will go on to the next page in her maths book in the next lesson, and several similar examples have been quoted.

Inappropriate next intentions appeared to be less a problem of teacher understandings of sequence and development, more a question of lack of awareness. This came out clearly when teachers were asked whether the children got out of the activity what they expected, where one comment in eight was of the type 'I didn't see the activity', 'I don't know, I was doing something else', 'I didn't see this activity, I was with other children'.

Nevertheless, when teachers were asked 'Did the children achieve what you expected?' and 'Was the activity a success or a failure?' many teachers felt able to respond whether or not they had seen it, as can be seen in Table 4.2.

Table 4.2

	Yes	Not sure	No
Did the children achieve what you expected?	79.6	12.4	8.0
	Success	Not sure	Failure
Was the activity a success or a failure?	93.4	4.4	2.2

Teachers claimed that their expectations were achieved in 80 percent of the activities. Where teachers indicated they were not sure, it was usually when they had not seen sufficient of the child during the task to comment. Often they said they would talk to the auxiliary before making a judgement. Seeing insufficient of the task to comment did not however stop them rating it a success or failure.

Teachers rated the overwhelming majority of their tasks a success, even when as indicated above, they had seen little of them. Success, however, was not rated in relation to their stated intentions, but mainly in relation to affective characteristics. The terms used include 'enjoyment', 'enthusiasm', 'absorbed', 'engrossed', 'gained satisfaction', 'interested', and, all too often, 'joined in, or achieved, at his/her own level'. Teachers seemed able to throw the most positive light on the situations they encountered. For example the teacher rated a success the activity where the child was constantly and deliberately breaking her pencil point on the grounds that she was obviously fascinated by what she was doing! The rare task rated a failure was usually characterised as a lack of involvement or a preoccupation with other things.

In short, activities were largely rated a success, even when not seen, mainly on the basis of indications of children's overt behaviour during teachers observational sweeps of the classroom, not on the basis of children's completed work, or judgement of it. In other words, behavioural rather than intellectual activity served as criteria, and because of this the quality of children's efforts was judged on criteria other than those stated in the teacher's intentions. And as in our other studies of infant teachers, busy work was often equated with appropriate or successful work.

5 Four Year Olds in School: Practice and Constraints

The context in which this study was carried out was one in which marked changes were taking place in the pattern of school admissions for four year old children, whereby 40 percent of them were entering into infant classes. The nursery educators, the losers in the battle for custom, had dubbed this movement as 'nursery education on the cheap' and, by their account, it was a pretty poor imitation of the real thing. They were supported in this view by HMI and DES, both of which had cast doubts on the ability of infant schools and teachers to deliver an appropriate and differentiated curriculum. Dire warnings were thus being issued about the likelihood of unnecessary distinctions between work and play, inappropriate introduction to formal skills and overlong days.

This debate about the what and where of the education of four year olds has proceeded largely in the absence of data on actual practice. Nevertheless it has to be said that studies which have been carried out, although exceedingly limited in size and scope, have tended to support the concerns expressed above. The other side of that coin, however, is that studies have also made it clear that the nursery educators themselves were not capable of achieving their own rhetoric – a classic case of pots calling kettles. Clark's (1988) call for studies to be undertaken to produce the evidence on the content and quality of provision was thus timely, since the debate, and any subsequent policy decisions, must surely be based on the reality rather than the rhetoric of infant practice.

Our aim for this study emanated from these concerns and were fourfold;

1   To ascertain the nature and quality of the learning experiences of four year olds in infant classes.
2   To identify those classroom and teacher activities which stimulated or maintained experiences of high quality.

3   To acquire the perspectives of head and class teachers on the education of such children.

4   To utilise insights gained from the study to influence pre- and in-service training.

No attempt was made to compare nursery and infant provision, nor to contrast the effect of differing LEA intake procedures. Both types of study can be fully justified but would have required a much bigger sample of LEAs, schools and children and thus a much bigger budget than was available to us.

The context for the classroom observations, which form the heart of the study, was characterised by interviewing heads and teachers in three LEAs, the findings of which provided little grounds for optimism. More than one half of the teachers interviewed had less than five years experience teaching this age range and only a quarter had actually been trained for it. And most teachers expressed dissatisfaction with the level of resourcing of the physical context of learning – equipment, materials, space and access, as well as of human resources. Clearest of all the findings concerned the differences between the teachers' stated aims and their curriculum priorities, whereby the former were dominated by affective, and the latter by cognitive, criteria.

These findings support those of other studies carried out in different parts of the country, so that the general picture of infant teachers struggling on valiantly in the face of adversity, being unable, for whatever reason, to reconcile their aims and practices, is likely to be an accurate one. However that struggle is not the main concern here, despite the debilitating effect it may have on the individual teacher. Rather it is the impact of that struggle on the quality of children's learning experiences, judged in relation to several indices of appropriateness – of activities to intentions, of presentation, of activity to child, of classroom organisation and of future intentions. The findings of the analyses of the 250 tasks observed, their inter-relationships, and possible causes and consequences, are now considered.

Curriculum and its presentation

It has been argued that content, and the purposes for which it is taught, are at the very heart of teaching–learning processes (Shulman, 1986). In other words tasks, and their associated intentions underpin classroom learning. In drawing out descriptions from the teachers on these issues we essentially asked the question 'Why this task for this child at this time?' In general teachers were able to state fairly clearly their intentions although some were less specific than others which made them difficult to analyse, and some operated with multiple intentions, not all of which were embodied in the activities planned. It is also undeniable that the links between some teachers' intentions and the activities planned were somewhat tenuous. Nevertheless in general teachers knew what they wanted to do and were able to plan accordingly. This leaves open the question of whether what they wanted to do was appropriate, but we were in no position, in this study, to posit or discuss what alternative intentions were possible, or what alternative activities existed for teachers' stated intentions. Nevertheless these are very important questions and ought to be discussed extensively in schools and training contexts, and we hope that the case studies portrayed in Chapter Six will aid this process.

Once activities are chosen they have to be presented in some way such that the demands are clearly specified so that children know what to do, and appropriate materials and other resources are available. Generally teachers were successful in this. Only one in six activities were inadequately presented, but some teachers were very much better at this than others. The most serious aspect of poor presentation observed was that too often teachers did not indicate, or indicated wrongly, to children the purpose of their activities. Picture sequencing canvassed as colouring and cutting, counting portrayed as playing with farm animals, and understanding shapes presented as colouring in, are all examples of this. The problem here is that the teacher's specification, or lack of it, confers importance on to certain demands and ignores others, ie it dictates the task situation. Thus, colouring in becomes the important activity, not the understanding of sequence or shape. This effect was quite clear from some of the interviews with the children.

This phenomenon is not, however, restricted to infant teachers, or indeed British teachers. Anderson et al (1984) studied American first grade classrooms and found that only five percent of all teacher presentations included 'explicit statements of content-related purpose, such as 'This will help you practice the new rules about sounding out words with 'ou' in the middle'. Roehler et al (1983) had also found that children who were given more explicit information about purpose and strategies articulated these more ably in post-task interviews, and these findings fit neatly into a theoretical consideration of the problem in terms of advance organisers (Ausubel, 1968). This theory holds that when meaningful knowledge is organised and presented in an orderly manner, students will learn more efficiently and effectively. Teachers should thus structure information that pupils are to encounter to provide an intellectual scaffold with which to acquire and fit the ideas and facts contained in it. The use of advance organisers will, Ausubel believes, improve understanding and motivation.

Roehler et al (1983) would make even further demands of teachers, including explicitness of presentation within a more general style of proactive teaching. They have argued that a proactive approach has the greatest potential for success, and define the approach as one in which teachers are themselves consciously aware of the function of the skill being taught and the linkages between these skills and the content to be processed, that they analyse a skill and identify the salient features of the mental processing one does when employing it, and that they actively teach students how to do the processing.

Lack of teacher clarity, and/or lack of teacher thought about clarity were certainly features of the classrooms we observed, leaving children unclear and unaware and thereby occasionally very anxious about task demands. And clarity extends from the presentation itself to the children's understanding of what is being presented. Being clear about an activity on caterpillars is of no avail if the child has an inadequate grasp of the concept of caterpillars. Here, however, we are drifting into the area of task appropriateness to which we will return later.

The provision of necessary materials was not a major problem in general, being apparent in one activity in six, but it had severe effects in a minority of classrooms. These included, in addition to the children being unable to complete their activities successfully, the loss of interest and involvement, with knock-on effects on classroom management through children wandering about, becoming noisy or demanding etc.

The quality of presentation is thus critical in providing the appropriate intellectual structure or scaffold for the activity, in defining demand, and in making available the necessary material resources and support. As such it can aid or hinder children's performances and achievements.

Activities can of course be perfectly presented but make inappropriate demands on children. The appropriateness of task to child, or 'match' as it is more commonly known, has been a particular focus in HMI reports, and research over the last decade. Judgements of match by HMI have been made only on the basis of observations of practice, whereas empirical studies have used a clearer theoretical rationale requiring post-task interviews with children to ascertain their understandings of activities completed. We found these interviews more difficult in this study because of the age of the children. Some four year old children have very few inhibitions with adults but others can be exceedingly shy, and in such cases there was no point in forcing the issue. Thus, even though our judgements on match were very reliable overall, there were cases when these judgements were of higher inference, and wherever there was a doubt the activity was deemed appropriate. The finding that one activity in four was inappropriate is thus a conservative one.

In the 250 activities observed there were more overestimates than underestimates, ie more activities were too difficult than too easy, and several examples of each were provided in Chapter Four. This situation pertained in most curriculum areas other than play, which was characterised by a high degree of pupil choice and by under-estimation; children tended to choose activities which were familiar, and in which there was little challenge.

Play

The view that the education of young children is founded on play has almost attained the status of a commandment, but it is a commandment observed far more in the telling than in the doing. This can be seen from previous studies, and our interviews with teachers, all of which indicate a marked discrepancy between stated aims and practice. Thus, in their interviews most teachers mentioned play in their aims, but only six percent of our observations were of play activities. Other studies tell the same story. Tizard et al (1988), for example, argued on the basis of their observations that the commonly-held view that infant schooling encouraged learning through discovery or play, was a myth.

The play which we observed was very limited and very limiting. The teachers appeared to have low expectations of it, often acting as a time filler, and far too frequently there was no clear purpose or challenge, a lack of pupil involvement, very little monitoring or attempt at extension. In other words, play activities tended not to provide learning experiences of acceptable quality.

How, given the central rhetorical role of play in early childhood education, does this state of affairs come about? Several interacting factors appear to be involved, including teachers' assumptions, their roles and expectations in play activities, classroom routines and lack of ancillary support.

It has already been argued that play tended to be used as a time filler, a strategy which allows teachers some freedom to do other things. Sestini (1987) notes the same practice:

Although several teachers said that they would like to spend more time involved in play, in practice, while groups of children were involved in play the teacher became free to focus upon hearing children read, to check writing and work on other completed tasks. Children did not elicit the teacher's involvement in their play.

She further argued that play served social functions in the classes and that most of it presented no cognitive challenge. She concluded:

Children's expectations of play in school were constrained, not only by limited resources, space and time, but also by their orientation to play as a peer group activity, not as an activity which promotes learning.

Adult involvement

Sestini's finding that the level of adult involvement was low in play activities was also apparent in our observations, indeed it is a common finding in studies of nursery and young infant children. Yet the value of adult presence and support is strongly emphasised in the research and theoretical literature. Bruner (1985) for example has found that adult presence 'strikingly increases the richness and length of play', whereas Sylva et al (1980) stressed interaction rather than just presence, finding that children in the age range 3½ to 5½ are 'more likely to engage in complex play when in the company of adults who were interacting with them, rather than merely in their presence'. Tyler et al (1979) have also investigated the impact of adults in nursery and reception classes and have argued that the effect is dramatic in harnessing and focusing children's attention:

> Learning cannot take place unless attention is paid to the relevant stimuli. Thus the adult plays a fundamental role in enabling the child to deploy its attention most effectively. In view of this the traditional practice of leaving children to learn through their own efforts seems a questionable one.

Tizard (1985) criticises 'traditional nursery education' on the same basis, ie that there is little stress on children learning from adults. She argues that the twin cornerstones of its pedagogy are learning through play and learning through socialisation with other children, branches of pedagogy which are weak in both theory and practice. Thus, in nursery schools, there are few of what she calls 'passages of intellectual search'.

The quality of teacher/adult intervention is critical to activities in all areas of the curriculum and is voiced most vividly in theoretical terms by Bruner and Vygotsky. Bruner portrays it in the following terms – 'One of the most crucial ways in which culture provides aid in intellectual growth is through a dialogue between the more experienced and the less experienced'. This echoes Vygotsky's (1962) earlier treatise that children often succeed in performing tasks and solving problems when helped by an adult which they would not have been able to do alone ie, 'a child's potential for learning is revealed and indeed is often realised in interactions with more knowledgeable others.... For Vygotsky, then, cooperatively achieved success lies at the foundations of learning and development' (Wood, 1988). Indeed Wood ventures that 'Four year olds can be taught to do tasks that, alone, they will not master until around age seven or eight. For them to learn, however, instruction must be geared to that (changing) level of competence. When this condition can be and is achieved, young children can be taught and do learn'.

It is unlikely however that these conditions can realistically be met in contemporary classrooms. We have seen that resources and social conditions place severe limits on teachers' actions, as indeed do their own conceptions of their role, and their own skills. We argued in Chapter Four that the amount and quality of adult intervention was poor, and part of this problem, and one keenly felt by teachers, was the lack of ancillary support.

We have found it necessary to comment adversely on the quality of much interaction between ancillaries and children, whereby opportunities were missed to increase children's knowledge or extend their thinking. The reasons for this are not difficult to find, reasons which have their source both inside and outside the classroom. Inside the classroom the communication between ancillaries and teachers was too often not planned, not explicit, indeed often not deemed to be necessary. Some teachers appeared to view the ancillary as a semi-autonomous surrogate teacher needing no inputs or explanations. How inappropriate this kind of relationship is is exhibited by Kevin's teacher who clearly demonstrates the enhanced quality of children's experiences through careful planning of children's activities, materials and resources, even to the extent of delineating the concepts and vocabulary, and communicating these demands fully to the ancillary. This teacher showed us what a high quality teacher-ancillary relationship looks like. But it is not one for the tired, the burned out or the faint hearted. It requires energy, commitment, enthusiasm, and the pedagogical skills necessary for that level of planning.

The problem outside the school is that even where ancillary help is provided, appropriate in-service training rarely is. It is appreciated that LEAs are not overflowing with INSET money, but now that the education of four year olds is a national priority area the time seems appropriate for some re-thinking on training. We have seen that the role of the auxilliary can be crucial both in classroom and task management terms and as such lack of training is surely a false economy. Perhaps it is now time for infant teachers to cast aside their gentle image and become more bullish, along the lines advocated by Wood et al (1980) who argued that

> we should not be bullied by political proclamations about the proper level of provision of teacher resources for the young child. Our yardstick should not be some politically or economically expedient half truth based on a convenient theory but one based on actual observations of the quality, depth and extent of contact between individual children and responsive adults in different situations.

Classroom management

Thus far we have been pondering the difficulties that teachers and other adults in the classroom have in providing appropriate cognitive interventions to aid children's learning, particularly in the task implementation stage. It would seem, from our observations, that the opportunities made available for these purposes were crucially dependent on the effectiveness of the classroom management strategies adopted, notably the level of teacher awareness, and classroom monitoring activity, both of which left room for improvement. Pupil involvement was often sporadic, caused by children wandering about, chatting, distracting others and generally increasing the noise level. And pupil interest could wane and boredom set in due to the lack of teacher presence. It is worth recording that interest and involvement appeared worse when task demands were unclear or where teacher expectations were low, such that the children knew that they could get by with minimal effort. Yet maintaining high levels of involvement and interest are critical in optimising children's present and future achievement. At nursery and infant level Tyler et al (1979) report that the effect of harnessing and focusing children's attention is dramatic, and in other studies interest and task orientation or involvement have been found to be the best predictors of achievement in later infant school (cf Perry, et al 1979). As William James argued at the end of the last century 'whether the attention comes by grace of genius or by dint of will, the longer one does attend to a topic, the more mastery of it one has' (1899).

We are keenly aware in making these criticisms that the demands on teachers' time in reception classes are enormous and that they cannot possibly be doing all things, and be in all places, at the same time. Nevertheless as Lemlech (1988) points out 'the teacher "pro" is constantly aware of what is happening in the classroom, and is attentive to instructional needs'. Although this may be an over-optimistic statement there are ways of maximising management behaviours to create time. Kounin (1970) for example indicates that the most salient teacher behaviours in maintaining pupil involvement include awareness of monitoring classroom events, the ability to maintain a smooth flow of events, particularly at points of transition, and the ability to deal with two or more things at the same time.

Assessment

One of the demands that teachers are increasingly going to have to create time for is assessment. Dowling (1988) has argued that this is an area that teachers of young children have traditionally shied away from, and the truth of that argument is amply supported by our findings. Assessment, and more importantly, diagnosis of children's understandings, were very noticeable by their absence, or were limited to brief encounters of an unsatisfactory kind. And as has been referred to already, expectations for the quality of children's completed work were low, just as Tizard et al (1988) found in ILEA infant schools, and for very similar reasons. They criticised the ILEA teachers for lack of clear objectives for what they intended children to learn: consequently, the teachers could not assess whether they themselves, or their children, had achieved the objectives. The teachers in our study did not lack intentions, but the judgements they brought to bear on children's work, when they were made, bore little relationship to their original intentions. Thus cognitive aims were judged an affective criteria. By this expedient they very rarely had to deem a task, or a child, a failure, since they were always able to find some aspect acceptable. It follows from this that almost every task could be judged a success, which is precisely what teachers did, irrespective of whether or not the child, or the work, had been seen.

But surely this is self-defeating? How can any teacher, of any child, of any age, who believes in the principle of individualisation justify the non-diagnosis of children's understandings? How can teachers decide on the next optimal step in the development of a child's potential or progression, in any curriculum area, without knowing that child's attainments?

These are not just statements of our own views. The Plowden Report talked of the necessity for detailed observations of individual children for matching their demands to children's stages of development, and underlined 'the importance of diagnosing children's needs and potentialities'. This was taken up in the HMI report Education 5–9 where they expressed the belief that a planned education requires the careful assessment of children's individual needs and the recording of their progress and development. They too found little evidence of such assessment. Frequent and careful assessment of children's abilities and attainments occurred in only 12 percent of schools.

Yet we know from our earlier studies just how important assessment and diagnosis is, and HMI (1980) have also linked these with matching:

Generally, schools that had good procedures for the assessment of individual children's needs, abilities and attainments were, not surprisingly, markedly more successful in providing appropriate work for their pupils than were those schools without such procedures.

In addition links have been made between assessment and young children's development. The latest study to show this concluded that 'teachers who examine the skills of the individual child and plan instructions accordingly are able to enhance the child's language development' (Lane and Bergan, 1988).

Planning instruction 'accordingly' is the rub, however. HMI (1980) found, as did we, that even when assessment was carried out little use was made of it. Where individual differences were revealed they were disregarded, and assessment was not used to adjust planned assignments. This pattern accords with our analyses that showed that teachers' next intentions very often were poorly related to children's performances because no clear assessment of these performances had been carried out.

We are aware from our extensive experience in developing and participating in in-service courses on diagnosis that it is very difficult to undertake in the maelstrom of classroom activities. Effective diagnosis requires skill in relating to children about their understandings and misconceptions of content, it requires an understanding on the part of teachers of subject matter; and of the structure of subject matter on which to base decisions about sequence and development. It requires a classroom management style which allows adequate time for the teacher to observe and relate to individual children without interruptions; it requires the pedagogical skills to then transform that diagnostic information gained into appropriate learning experiences. So formidable are these demands that they have led some writers to despair. Wood (1988), for example, writes

Teachers are also expected to be capable of diagnosing the needs of the individual learner and to know how to meet them once discovered. In my less optimistic moments I wonder whether such demands can possibly be considered realistic when one adult is asked to achieve all these ends in the service of 20, 30 or perhaps 40 children in a classroom.

And Desforges and Cockburn (1987) argue that since 'diagnostic work is extremely difficult to conduct in the classroom as presently conceived, it seems little more than a researcher's self-indulgence to prescribe it'.

We understand, but do not subscribe to, such despair. We marvel at the complexities of classroom processes, and at the high level of skills and knowledge that teachers require to orchestrate that complexity effectively, just as we marvel at the complexities of space travel. But despair did not get us into space, and neither will it improve teaching and learning. So what is the way forward? Firstly let us be clear about the major points needing consideration.

Improving teaching and learning

The picture we have painted is of teachers striving valiantly in the face of adversity, and in the face of official ambivalence. The major teaching problems we have delineated, including poor specification of the purpose of activities, low expectations, poor matching, inadequate monitoring and a neglect of assessment and diagnosis, are not problems peculiar to infant class teachers. Our studies of teachers of four to 14 year olds all show the same pattern. It is endemic. It may be that some of these difficulties are more apparent among infant classes simply because of the characteristics of the children at a particular stage in their development, allied perhaps with the more active nature of the curriculum.

We are here criticising teaching, not teachers. It would be unfair to saddle teachers with the whole responsibility for the above, since these same areas tend to be neglected in teacher education courses both at pre- and in-service levels. The truth of this statement can be judged against a reading of the HMI document *The New Teacher in School* (1988). In it, HMI reported that 30 percent of tasks were mismatched, with the usual pattern of under- and overestimation: in approximately one task in five planning and preparation were poor – in which teachers 'failed to consider purpose', and 'had not established clear objectives'; and in one quarter of cases marking of children's work was unsatisfactory. Teachers were unclear about the diagnostic purposes of marking and 'there was insufficient analysis of children's responses to ascertain their level of understanding and determine the next step'. It all sounds very familiar.

Two things become plain. Teacher educators have some reflecting to do on the quality of their courses, and secondly, any suggestions that we might make for improvement will apply equally to all teachers, not just to those teaching the youngest children in schools.

Some will be easier to implement than others. Take, for example, the use of advance organisers to improve the specification of the purpose of activities by scaffolding children's thoughts and perceptions. The implementation of this far from new idea requires no change in classroom practice, other than a modification in the way teachers plan and think about their task intentions and justifications, and then verbalise these at a level suitable for children. This description over-simplifies, but the point to note is that a massive change in practice is not necessary for an initiative which could have profound effects on children's understandings.

Implementing other improvements will require a much more radical restructuring of teachers' philosophies, thoughts and actions, but fortunately the major problems of matching, monitoring and assessment can be tackled together. We have argued that at the root of poor matching is inadequate diagnosis (Bennett et al, 1984), and this has been supported by HMI surveys. We have also argued that diagnosis cannot routinely be carried out in classrooms, even where teachers have the relevant skills, until more appropriate forms of classroom organisation are set in place. We have dubbed typical classroom practice 'crisis management' whereby teachers attempt to be the providers of instant solutions to a constant stream of problems. This has been shown to be a singularly inappropriate form of organisation since it devours teacher time, thereby denying opportunities for observation and monitoring of the class. The problems of matching, monitoring and diagnosis are thus intertwined, and all occur as a consequence of teachers' persistence in attempts to implement and maintain a philosophy of individualisation. It is this which is the core of the problem. And the reason is simple. Individualisation is impossible.

Some may recoil from this statement, whereas for others it will be a self-evident fact. It was certainly a view held by the Plowden Committee. They subscribed to the principle of individualisation but admitted it was not possible. 'Sharing out teachers' time is a major problem. Only 7 or 8 minutes a day would be available for each child if all teaching were individual. Teachers therefore have to economise by teaching together a small group of children who are roughly at the same stage'. This line of thinking can be traced through HMI reports ever since. The 1978 survey blamed poor matching of the more able children on the difficulties teachers had when every child in the class is engaged on a different activity. In the report on 5–9 year old children, HMI stated

> Where children were given too little help in organising their work the quality of what was done suffered to some extent because many worked too often as individuals rather than as members of a group. Individual work, when overdone, allows the teacher little time to discuss difficulties with the children in more than a superficial way, and provides too few opportunities for the children to learn from each other. (1980)

Other researchers are more specific. Galton et al (1980) for example asserted, from their findings, that

... the Plowden prescripts stressing discovery learning and the probing, questioning character of the teacher's role appear, at least with present class sizes, impossible of achievement.

Finally, Topping (1988) in more avuncular mood, wrote

for one teacher with a class of 30 pupils to serve as an efficient and effective direct educator is frankly impossible, as any teacher who has desperately tried to hear every member of a primary school class reading every day will readily agree. All too often this ends up with one child reading to the teacher, while another dozen wait at the teacher's desk for attention in respect of other problems; administrative interruptions and problems with deviant behaviour compound the awfulness of the situation. Omniscience is not a contractual requirement. Teachers must increasingly function as managers of effective learning, rather than the font of all available wisdom.

Many readers will have made the connection between these statements, stressing group activities and teacher and peer talk, with the theoretical positions, outlined earlier, of Bruner and Vygotsky. Their theoretical insights have been very influential in shifting our conceptions of young children's learning which, in turn, have clear implications for the way we, as educators, conceptualise classroom processes and the teachers role in them. Bruner and Haste (1987) characterise this shift as a quiet revolution whereby children are now being considered as 'social beings' rather than as 'lone scientists'.

... It is not only that we have begun to think again of the child as a social being – one who plays and talks with others, learns through interactions with parents and teachers – but because we have come once more to appreciate that through such social life, the child acquires a framework for interpreting experience, and learns how to negotiate meaning in a manner congruent with the requirements of the culture.... 'Making sense' is a social process; it is an activity that is always situated within a cultural and historical context.
Before that, we had fallen into the habit of thinking of the child as an 'active scientist', constructing hypotheses about the world, reflecting upon experience, interacting with the physical environment and formulating increasingly complex structures of thought. But this active, constructing child had been conceived as a rather isolated being, working alone at her problem-solving. Increasingly we see now that, given an appropriate, shared social context, the child seems more competent as an intelligent social operator than she is as a 'lone scientist' coping with a world of unknowns.

Their message is clear – we need to move from individualistic to cooperative endeavour in our classrooms and in so doing open up new and exciting possibilities for the more effective management of classrooms and of learning.

But, you might argue, we already do groupwork. Whatever perceptions teachers might have about this, all the research evidence points in one direction. Children certainly sit *in* groups, but very rarely do they work *as* a group. Groups as presently organised are no more than physical juxtapositions of children working on individual tasks. There is virtually no real, cooperative groupwork happening in British classrooms (Bennett, 1987; Tizard et al, 1988; Galton et al, 1980). There is, on the other hand, a mass of evidence, particularly from the United States, which attests to the benefits of cooperative group work, including enhanced achievement, improved self-esteem and decreased racial stereotyping (cf Slavin, 1983).

There is also the likelihood of substantial gain of teacher time. No longer does the teacher take on the role as the font of all knowledge, or the first port of call, for the inevitable spelling or other such query. The group takes this responsibility. This releases valuable teacher time for monitoring and diagnosis. So why, given all these likely advantages, is so little cooperative group work happening? It requires a shift in teacher philosophy, away from the blinkers of individualisation, and a casting off of old habits and routines. This represents no mean feat, because no human being abandons the security of established practices lightly, and particularly when, as in this case, there is very little specific advice for teachers about how to organise such work. And it should be stressed that implementation is unlikely to be straight-forward – it demands changes in the teacher's role, in classroom organisation, and in the form and design of curriculum activities.

There is much work to be done here, all the more so now that there are attainment targets for skills in cooperation and communication to be built into the national curriculum documents. Such work is going ahead. As this chapter is being written we are instituting a research project on the implementation of cooperative learning as a part of a larger research programme on teacher education (Bennett and Wragg, 1989).

We have concentrated on cooperative learning here because it reflects con-temporary theories of children's learning and holds the promise of overcoming some of the major problems we have highlighted. This is not to deny the efficacy of other initiatives in overcoming other areas of difficulty. We would pick out in particular parental involvement schemes, which have demonstrated their value in children's learning, and which could be extended more formally into classroom assistance providing that adequate in-school training could be provided. We would also agree with Tizard et al (1988) that infant teachers should, as a matter of priority, be afforded non-contact time. A constant concern is that the demands on the infant teacher's time leaves insufficient room for reflection on their own practice, and as important, the discussion and evaluation of the practice of others. This, in part, is why we present, in the next chapter, a complete description of a half day's session for six different children, chosen to highlight important facets of our findings. We hope that teachers will find them a valuable resource and will take the opportunity to discuss them with colleagues either within or without formal in-service occasions.

In conclusion we need to make some response to the question posed in our title: *A good start?* We cannot be unequivocal about this, since for some children it proved an excellent start, yet for others it did not. It will probably always be thus. One of the givens of the British educational system is variation, particularly in the quality of teaching approach and curriculum cover. Tizard and her colleagues have shown this most recently with the finding that the school factors most responsible for infant children's differential progress were the teacher, and the activities she provided. And this kind of variation is unlikely to be much affected by implementation of the national curriculum. We have already indicated that variation could be diminished and the level of teaching quality enhanced by improved pre- and in-service teacher education, but this is true for all teachers. Factors which bear specifically on the quality on infant class practice tend largely to be outside the teacher's control. LEAs must now begin to debate the issue of the four year old in school more urgently, and attempt to throw off the mantle of ambivalence and seeming indifference. If a decision is made to continue the system then it needs appropriate resourcing, including adequate capitation, ancillary assistance and training. Too often, it would seem, political rhetoric hides classroom realities, and teachers are sacrificed to economic expediency.

Head teachers too have some difficult decisions to make. It is they who apparently allowed the movement to gain momentum, and it is they who, in the absence of clear LEA policies, must decide whether it should be maintained or wound down. Head teachers are, of course, in a classic compromise situation. On the one hand schools are increasingly in a market economy, and, as the churches and banks have learned, it pays to get your future customers in early. On the other hand it may be that the situation in the school would make a decision to enter four year olds less than optimal for teacher and children. In such circumstances we would argue for care and caution. The first year of schooling is critical for children. It has to be as good as we can make it.

PART TWO

Case studies

6   Improving Practice

What we have presented in the previous chapters is a characterisation of the strengths and weaknesses of current practice, a necessary pre-requisite, in our view, to the achievement of improvement in that practice. Strategies aimed at such improvements can take many forms. One way is to present the outcomes of research and theory to teachers, based on which are suggestions for changes in practice. This is the focus we took in the previous chapter where we argued for a movement toward more cooperative endeavours in classrooms. This mode, which we might call the 'outside-in' approach, holds the possible advantage of enriching practice with theory, but has the disadvantage of lacking clear guidance for teachers on implementation. An alternative is to use descriptions of specific practices to highlight the strengths and weaknesses more generally apparent, a mode we might call the 'inside-out' approach. This has the advantage of being grounded in classroom realities and thus makes sense to teachers. Its disadvantage is that analyses can be undertaken which are uninformed by theory and research. Ideally therefore a combination of the inside-out and outside-in approaches is required. It is this combination which we have tried to achieve in this, and the previous chapter.

Chapter Five presented an overview of our study and related the findings to earlier investigations, prior to a consideration of explanations and improvements. In contrast this chapter presents descriptions of practice, appropriately contextualised. More specifically we present six half-day sessions chosen to highlight particular aspects of practice. Each case study is complete, ie it contains information on the school, class and child, the teacher's intentions and task presentation, a record of the child's activity, and information from the interviews with the child and the teacher. Following each case study some guidelines for discussion are provided.

We have found in our in-service courses that case studies of this kind generate enormous interest and enthusiasm which is reflected in the depth and quality of the discussions which follow. Although we would hope that individual teachers will read these and reflect on the nature of their own practice, we think there is great benefit to be had from sharing reactions, analyses and reflections with other teachers within or without their school. Our hope also is that cooperative ventures of this kind would be shared with ancillary assistants, and parents who help in the school. We have shown that insufficient support is available for such people and believe that these case studies could provide the structure for that support.

Our final hope therefore is that the names of Adrian, Karen, Kevin, Mandy, Roger and Ryan will become familiar wherever pre-service or in-service courses on four year olds in school are held.

Adrian

This session is observed during Adrian's first week at a primary school which is situated between a private housing estate and council houses. It is a working class area and the private houses would be classified as 'starter homes'. There are 36 children in the class and the age span is 4+ to 6.8. There is very little space available in the classroom because of the number of tables and chairs. The children are seated at these for most of their activities. There is a small home corner, also sand and water trays but these are very rarely used. There is no book corner or carpeted area.

The school day usually begins with assembly. The children are expected to attend this as soon as they start school because 'It is school policy that the children learn to sit and listen as soon as possible'.

(The teacher was aware that she was not coping with the youngest children and asked for extra help. Although this was given, some members of staff thought it was unnecessary. Because she was so obviously under stress the observer offered to discontinue the visits. However, the school staff – including the classteacher – wanted the study to continue.)

The teacher describes Adrian as being a confident child. He is boisterous which she feels may be a problem as he gets older.

Teacher's intentions for Adrian, with her activity descriptions, reasons and expectations.

Activity 1

Description	– *Patterns*, using circles
Reasons	– They are going to make them into caterpillars
Expectations	– An understanding of the circle shape

Activity 2

Description	– *Handwriting*
Reasons	– To improve their left to right coordination. Manual dexterity – using pencils

Expectations   – To help to learn to form letters properly. Some will have had a lot of experience with pencils, some not

Activity 3

Description   – *PE*
Reasons   – We do it every week. It is timetabled and the apparatus put out ready
Expectations   – Getting used to climbing and using their muscles. Improving coordination.

Activity log

(All class 35; 4.6–6.6; pre-activity)

11 new children came in on Monday, two days ago (Adrian being one of them). The teacher tells me they are awful – lots of tears and crying for Mummy – even at five past nine! It is getting her down. The room seems crowded with tables and chairs.

8.55   Children start to come in because it is raining. Usually they have to wait in the playground until the bell goes. The teacher is writing on the blackboard for the older ones, she occasionally comments to a child. One new child cries. The teacher is talking to another parent and takes no notice. The parent helper goes to the child and distracts him with drawing.

9.00   A child goes to the teacher holding up his arms and crying. 'Sit down,' she says, pushing him towards his table. He sits by the helper who reaches for him. Three children are crying now by the parent helper. All need her arms, she tries to touch them all. The teacher shouts at a boy, 'John, that is enough, we'll all cry in a minute'. She tells him off. A boy is dragged into the classroom by the teacher. The teacher and the helper go out leaving three crying, one is holding the helper's hand when she comes back.

9.06   The teacher says sharply 'All line up by the door'. She claps her hands. Two crying children are dragged screaming into the line, one forced to leave his new pencil case on the table.
    T: 'Stop that, you're a big boy now.'

Assembly About learning at school. The children enjoyed two songs. The new ones are in the second row, two are crying quietly.
('They have to learn to come into assembly,' said a senior member of staff.) The infant classes are told they will have to undress after play 'to have apparatus'. A new girl cries.

9.45   *Register*
    T: 'After play we're doing apparatus – it's good isn't it, going to PE?'
    A child cries, she's told off. No other explanation about PE.

Teacher says some will be going to the Remedial teacher as yesterday, she gives their names.

T: 'Older children first, first of all put your hand up if you can tell me what that is about . . . in letterland.' She holds up a card.

Four children go out with another teacher.

The teacher is talking about the letterland characters. She talks about words beginning with W, asks the children for words. All the children are sitting near her on the carpet, some on the floor between the tables and chairs because of the shortage of space.

T: 'What I want you to do is draw me a big picture of the Wicked Water Witch and the Hairy Hat Man, her knocking off his hat, then on the other side of the paper do the writing to go with it.'

A new child: 'Teacher I don't know how to do that'.

T: 'You're not doing that, if you'd listened, I said it was for the older ones.'

To another crying new child who said something 'No you're not doing this yet, you're not old enough.'

T: 'Get on with your work.'

Activity 1 (6; 4b 2g; 4.6–4.11; teacher-chosen)

10.00   T: 'New ones, stay sitting down here. We're going to Mrs P and make a caterpillar. Go and sit down on this table.'

T: 'In my bag here I've got all sorts of circles, you can choose whatever colours you like. Start to choose some colours while I get them out.'

10.15   Parent goes out to find some sugar paper for them to use. Group round one table covered with newspaper, others on another table. Tables covered with newspaper, with 2 tubs of glue, brushes and spatulas. The parent gives out large grey paper, there is not enough room on the table, she finds some newspaper and moves some to the next table.

Adrian to me: 'We have to stick it together like that, we're going to make some nice things for my Mum, but teacher said I can't take it home.'

Ancillary to a boy: 'No caterpillars go in a line, don't they'. She rearranges his circles.

The paste is very stiff, it sticks to the brush in lumps.

Ancillary: 'Keep them in a nice line.'

Adrian: 'There's the wings.' Putting tissue paper on so it flaps about.'

Ancillary: 'Your caterpillar is going up in the sky, it doesn't do that.'

She re-arranges it into line and sticks some more on for him.
Ancillary: 'Can you draw some legs on?'
Ancillary draws feelers on Adrian's caterpillar. She asks him to draw some like hers. (She meant over hers.) He draws set of feelers on the next circle.
Adrian is still talking about wings on his paper.
Ancillary: 'Can you write your name?'
He writes some letters – some are in his name.
Ancillary writes his name: 'Can you copy this?'
He copies four letters, then: 'I can't do this one.'
Ancillary helps him do two more letters.
The teacher gives them felt pens for doing legs.
Ancillary: 'Oh, we're using felt pens are we?'
Adrian: 'Done it, teacher.' Holding paper up.
He gets up and gets his pencil case. He has drawn a curly feeler on the head of the caterpillar.
Ancillary: 'Would you like to go over that with felt pen?'
Adrian draws curly feelers on the second segment.
Another boy writes J on Adrian's paper.
Child: 'Show Miss Brown.'
Adrian: 'I did.'
Adrian to teacher: 'Are we going out there?'
T: 'I don't know ... if it's raining. ...'
Adrian watches the teacher helping a child at his table.

Activity 2 (6, 4b 2g; 4.6–4.11; teacher-chosen)

Worksheets are given out by ancillary and teacher as children finish caterpillars.
T: 'Join up all the dots on the caterpillar ladybird.'
Teacher leaves.
Adrian starts, he doesn't know what to do. He draws in the spaces.
T: 'Round the circles – do that one.' (Hurriedly putting her finger on a circle.)
T: To others: 'You should be on this table doing this now, come on.'
Adrian: 'I can colour the feet in.'
Adrian: 'Poor ladybird, he's grumpy. You're not allowed to go in there though (the centre).'
Ancillary gives Adrian a crayon: 'Colour in the spots black, then do the body red.'
Adrian: 'Have I done it yet, all over it?'
Ancillary: 'No just round his spots.'
Adrian shows a boy what's in his pencil case. He gets a ruler out and draws straight lines on the paper. A child draws on his paper, helping him. Ancillary tells him not to – he must do his own.
Adrian scribbles on the last legs.
Me: 'Did you have to round the circle one way, this way, or that way?'

Adrian: 'It don't matter. Can you do my name? Adrian Green.'
I suggest he asks the teacher.
He goes and talks to a boy who is starting his snack.

Wet playtime. The teacher says they can look at a book, draw a picture but no toys out. Three older children come in, to supervise wet play.
Adrian gets some paper from the teacher to draw.

Activity 3 (All class; 4.6, 6.6; teacher-chosen)

11.00 T: 'Older ones, get your shoe bags.'
Adrian dashes out the door, he's stopped by the parent.
T: 'Right, you children (new ones) go and get your shoe bags off your pegs.'
A girl starts crying, one boy can't find his bag.
T: 'Right, shoes off, take your tie off.'
Adrian takes his shoes off, he takes his T-shirt out of his bag.
The children change where they can, by their chairs. It seems very cramped. The parent helps the new ones.
A boy helps Adrian undo his tie. Adrian plays with his tie.
One new boy stands, holding his bag, not watching, he looks grey, blank faced.
Two older boys are teasing Adrian, he seems to be enjoying it. They seem to be telling him to take his pants off.
The teacher and the parent help the children. The others wait by the door, some in leotards, some in underwear.
The crying girl is undressed by the parent. A boy undoes some of Adrian's shirt button, another helps. Adrian jumps up and down and gets told off by the teacher.

11.10 Adrian struggling with his shirt, one button still done up.
The teacher forcibly undresses a crying, struggling child. This creates quite a commotion. Adrian doesn't take much notice.
The parent comes to help Adrian, takes off his shirt, puts his clothes away. She puts on his plimsolls.

11.12 They go into hall, just down the corridor. The parent is still helping Adrian. He follows.

11.14 All sitting on the floor in the hall except one crying boy who is in the classroom with the parent. She carries him in crying.
The teacher directs the children to particular apparatus. She tells the one who is crying that he can join in when he takes his trousers off. He has forgotten his shorts.
Adrian goes with a group of seven to a bench with a mat either end. They stand on one mat, then run along bench and jump off onto mat. Adrian enjoys this.
Other apparatus – climbing bars, ropes, two vaulting horses, a small climbing frame and sloping bench, five pieces of apparatus. Everything seems very

crowded and close together.

Adrian runs along the bench, he is confident, a bit awkward, but he is thoroughly enjoying it. He rushes along the bench like a rocket, 1-2-3-4-5-6-7-8-9 and jumps. He is told by adult not to go like that.

11.20 T: 'All sit down.' Adrian sits on the PE mat. The teacher asks the older girls if they would like to go on the ropes.

Adrian gets up and tells her he would like to go on the large climbing frame. She sends him there.

Adrian climbs up the climbing frame, a high one. He climbs up and over half way, about 7 or 8 feet, talking to a boy. His movements are a little immature, but he climbs without fear, up and down again.

The parent comes and talks to him.

'Have you climbed all the way up there?'

He laughs and smiles: 'Yes.'

He climbs down and falls off awkwardly, he looks startled, but climbs again.

Adrian: 'I am the . . . in the world.'

He is at the top, shouting at some children.

11.30 T: 'Right, get off the apparatus, now.'

He does, two new ones don't. He rubs his shoes on the bars, they squeak.

Teacher is listening to a message from a teacher.

Teacher chooses a leader for the girls. Two new boys go to join their line and are dragged back.

'You're not a girl.'

Adrian lines up behind the boys.

11.35 Adrian: 'I can't find my bag.'

T: 'I don't know where you put it, look over there.'

He goes to look. He says to me politely, 'Can you see my bag anywhere? It says Adrian Green.'

I send him to the helper who put it on a chair. He gets his clothes and bag and starts to get dressed. There is hardly room to stand and get changed and it is difficult to move around the room.

An older girl comes to ask if any children need help.

Adrian dressed fairly easily, with a little help. He swings his bag round. He wanders to the far corner, talks to boys who pretend to fight him. He puts the bag tape round his head, over his eyes, then over his neck, talking and pointing and asking children, 'Does this look funny?'

11.50 Adrian wanders round the room, talking to children and looking at what they are doing, some are getting on with their work. He asks them things. He goes near a table occupied by older children and looks at some toys on the table belonging to a child.

The teacher tells him to hang his shoe bag up. He goes out. The teacher tells the children to get on with their work.

Activity unplanned

Adrian comes in jumping, he wanders, asks a boy what he is doing. He says he's not allowed to use the big felt pen. He takes a pen and goes off and comes back with some paper. He sits down at the wrong table and draws.

Other new children are wandering about, looking in cupboards or at the bricks. Adrian draws on a small, torn piece of paper – an older girl draws for him. The other new ones are working in their maths workbooks. The have to ring the objects of the same colour.

11.58 T: 'Put your books away' to the new ones. They do and are told to get their coats.

Adrian is still at the table with the older ones, drawing.

The new ones bring in their coats, a boy tells Adrian to get his coat. He looks up and goes out, putting his drawing on the top of a cupboard. The children go out to the Mums. Some go home. The helper is there. Adrian's Mum asks the teacher if she got his word book.

T: 'Yes.' To children: 'I didn't tell anyone to go.'

Too late. One child has run out and was halfway down the road. The parent had to go after him.

Interviews with child

Activity 1 Involvement was average and so was his enjoyment. He did not have a clear concept of caterpillars. He could easily stick shapes on when it was clear what was wanted.

Activity 2 He did the activity cheerfully, and with imagination! He had not understood the demand which subverted the teacher's intention. When questioned he did not know the circle had to be gone round in one way, did not understand the significance of the arrows indicating this, or that the dotted lines should be followed.

Activity 3 Highly involved, energetic, enjoyed it. Was confident in his capabilities to do the activities demanded.

Interview with teacher

Did the child get out of the activity what you expected?

Activity 1 They weren't very good. Some did them nicely, others didn't. Some stuck the circles on all over the paper instead of in a line.

Activity 2 The parent dealt with that. She gave him the sheet when she saw me doing it with the others. He's starting to get the idea.

Activity 3 I didn't notice him much. He was all right. He seemed quite confident.

Was it a success/failure? Why?

Activity 1 Yes. It's a logical way of doing it. He was following the instructions quite well.

Activity 2 I'm not that pleased. I should have provided a sheet with fewer things on it.

Activity 3 No, I've had better ones. Not all the apparatus was out, there were too many in one group at a time.

In the light of this, what will you do next?

Activity 1 I'll get them to draw round a circle by themselves and colour it in. They'll practise circles, writing the word circles over my writing, and cut out pictures in magazines of clocks, etc.

Activity 2 More handwriting practice using words this time, simple words with dots they have to join up, simple words, even if it's their name, or 'Mummy' etc.

Activity 3 Yes, the same kind of thing, the apparatus is put out for us. It must get monotonous for the children by the time they get to the last class.

Guidelines for discussion

1   List the evidence of teacher stress and its counter-productive effect on the children. What appear to be the reasons for this stress?

2   From the *Activity log* list the number of negative and positive signals given by the adults to the children. Do any implications follow from your findings?

3   This is Adrian's first week in school. In this context discuss the teacher's choice of activities and the overall balance achieved. Comment particularly on the teacher's choice of activities to fulfil her intentions, the way in which the activities are presented (including materials), and the quality of ancillary help.

4   The teacher is aware that she is not coping adequately. What advice would you offer her regarding her approach and style of management?

Karen

The school which Karen attends is not housed in a modern building but the general ambience is attractive, colourful and well maintained. There are child-centred displays and areas of interest in the corridors, the children are drawn from an affluent area of mixed old and new private housing. Many of the parents are professionals and it is an area of high employment. Karen has been attending part-time for six months.

The classroom is large, well-equipped, and is organised into small areas. The teacher prepares the session carefully and has a calm manner. The children enjoy a well-ordered learning environment and work happily within it.

The teacher describes Karen as a quiet child who spends a lot of time observing. She seems to be progressing well and has settled happily into school.

Teacher's intentions for Karen, with her activity descriptions, reasons and expectations.

Activity 1

Description	– *Change library books*
Reasons	– Awareness of books
Expectations	– Pleasure. Awareness and appreciation of books

Activity 2

Description	– *Drawing or writing* – about their books
Reasons	– Awareness of books. Development of activity 1
Expectations	– Increased awareness and appreciation

Activity 3

Description	– *Choice*
Reasons	– So that I can work with another group, and see the result of my input of maths and language activities
Expectations	– It depends what she does. Some coordination skills – a sense of achievement. She will use it to her level.

Activity 4

Description	– *Maths – partitioning sets*
Reasons	– Last time she was confused with 1:1 matching. My fault – I introduced it too quickly. It wasn't established.
Expectations	– Practice at partitioning

Activity Log

The children come into the classroom in ones and twos, able to talk to the teacher who is available, waiting for them.

9.00   Register. A birthday and assembly.

Activity 1/2 (All Class, 33; 4.6–5.0; teacher-chosen)

9.45   The children get their coats to go and get library books. The teacher gives them their library tickets – the parent has checked these – and they go across the playground to the library. This is an extremely cold spare classroom.
  Karen looks at the books on the shelves, picks up one or two, moves around. Then picks up a *Topsy and Tim* book.

9.55   T: 'If you've chosen your book, just sit down quietly and have a look at it.'
  The teacher has to stamp all the books. She has to deal with a difficult child, so the parent helper takes over the stamping.
  Karen joins the queue.
  Karen: 'Mr P. We've got *Topsy and Tim*'
  Karen (to me): 'I've chosen *Topsy and Tim*. My Mummy always buys *Topsy and Tim* at the library.'
  Karen shows me the date stamp in the front of the book, she knows that has something to do with it.
  Karen: 'I always get *Topsy and Tim* because it goes in my satchel.'
  (It's a small book.)
  Karen: 'Mummy and Daddy take it in turns to read to me, just before I go to bed.'

10.05   Back in the classroom, all in the book corner.
  T: 'Where do we find out what the book is about?
    The book is by . . .
    and the pictures are by . . . . .'
  She talks about the cover of the book, the title etc. Then she reads the story, occasionally stopping to comment and letting the children say something, but otherwise not allowing them to interrupt the flow of the story.
  The teacher explains very carefully what they will have to do.
  T: 'Have a good look at the book you have chosen. Then take a piece of paper (she shows them folded sugar paper a bit like a book), I want you to draw something that's on the front of your book.'
  Child: 'Do we have to write?'
  T: 'You can copy the writing if you can, but some writing may be difficult and you don't have to. Then I want you to look inside and find out something about it. How can we find out about it? Why did you choose it?'
  She asks several children and listens to their replies.

10.18   The children sit down in their special places and the teacher gives out the paper (Karen now in group of 4, 2b 2g)
  T: 'Put it down like a book.'
  Karen looks through the book very carefully. She looks at the front of it and starts to colour the paper matching the green background to the title.
  Karen: 'I can't do the writing, can I? I can't do the writing on the green, they won't see it.'

She starts to find the colours in the rest of the picture.

Karen: 'Red and blue, then yellow' (looking at the book).

'Now I have to do Topsy and Tim.'

She draws the patches of colour on her paper to match their position on the front of the book, but they are much smaller. She takes a pencil to draw Topsy and Tim.

Karen to another child: 'You've got lots of picture to do and I've finished!'

She calls to another child: 'I've got Topsy and Tim.'

The children discuss one boy's book – there is a witch-like figure on the front. Two others come and look at it.

Karen writes, copying from the book –

Topsy and Tim's new playground

She puts her fingers between the words as she writes.

10.30   The teacher comes to listen to the children telling her about their book.

T: 'Are you ready to tell me about your book?

Karen is pleased with her finished work. The teacher writes Karen's name and then writes inside, to Karen's dictation.

My book I chose it because I like Topsy and Tim book.

It's called Topsy and Tim's new garden

T: 'Which word says Topsy, do you know?'

Karen shakes her head: 'No.'

They play with their swing and slide

10.35   Playtime

Activity 3

(Children can choose from small toys – coloured shapes, playpax, flower cards, Unifix, pegs and pegboards, classification cards and picture dominoes.)

10.55   The children come in after play and sit down with their toys. The teacher tells the group who were playing with the toys to go and do their work on their library books.

Karen, playing on the floor, helps the parent to put away a box of toys.

Helper to Karen: 'While I'm playing with Tony, you play with Laura, I can't play with two at the same time.'

Karen plays with the multi-link cubes, fitting them together.

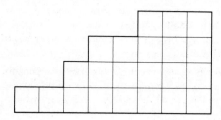

She tries to put a long piece on at right angles and eventually succeeds but it falls off and she tries again. Karen concentrates on fixing the cubes together and does not talk to others. She stops after a few minutes, breaks up her construction and puts it in the box.

11.05 The teacher asks another group to sit down and do their work. Karen, however, can carry on. She starts playing with the Unifix. She fits the cubes together in a long line. She holds it up smiling 'Who . . .'. It breaks and she tries to jam it back in the box. She stops to listen to the helper who is talking to nearby children about tidying up.

Karen holds her two pieces together to make a bridge for N to drive his motor cycle through.

Karen's pieces are the same length.

Karen: 'I've made walky legs. They are the same.

I wanted them to be the same.'

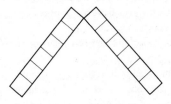

Karen walks around with the pieces now joined together, then goes to the box with a girl and takes some more pieces.

Karen: 'There's two more there.'

Girl: 'People I don't like I'm going to send on holiday. I'm going to send R on holiday. She's the one on your table I don't like.'

Karen does not respond. She fits cubes on her two rods, first on one, then the other, keeping them the same length.

Karen: 'They're the same. Yes they're the trousers.'

Karen: 'And it's getting bigger – look at those, they're getting more and more bigger . . . watch out, watch out. Mine is getting taller than yours' (to girl) (it wasn't).

Karen: 'Let go of it, I'll hold it.'

She grabs the girl's rod, but doesn't hold it and the girl's long rod falls and breaks.

Karen: 'Molly, polly it's a ————— dolly?'

Girl: 'Mine is the biggest' (it is).

Karen: 'Look at this. Mine is getting more and more bigger' (laughs)

The other girl has some pegs now.

Girl: 'I've got lots of sweeties, you've only got one sweetie.'

Karen takes no notice. Then she looks in the empty box.

Karen: 'Oh, you've got all the mostest. Look at mine.'

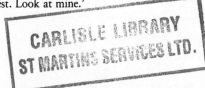

She holds her two long rods up. She 'walks' them across the carpet. One breaks, she has to mend it twice. She takes it to the helper.

Karen: 'Look Mr P.'

Me: 'How did you make them exactly the same?'

Karen: 'I started off with 1-1, 2-2, 3-3, then right up to the top.' (She points to each leg in turn as she speaks.)

Karen takes the rods to the teacher.

T: 'Tell me about these, then.'

Karen: 'They're the legs.'

T: 'Why are they the same height, you matched them up did you? Can you tell me about the blocks, are there more in one than the other?'

Karen tells her something I can't hear.

11.30   Karen puts the blocks away, they are breaking now, she goes to the peg box, but she can't have a pegboard, there isn't one spare. She wanders among the other toys, looking for something to play with, she jigs about, goes to her table, looks at a library book, then comes back to the pegs.

Karen: 'Come, we'll play with these.'

Girl: 'These can be chocolates, get some chocolates. They're very yummy and tasty.'

Karen: 'I'll get some sweeties instead.'

Girl: 'That's a flower, not a sweetie.' Karen laughs pretending to eat all the chocolate from girl's rod. Girl grabs it, stopping her, and puts some in the box.

Karen: 'We've got to do that big long line, haven't we?'

Girl: '. . . sweeties.'

Activity 4 (All class minus 8 (25); teacher-chosen)

11.35   After some tidying up, eight children go out for some drama work, the rest are all sitting by teacher, who is explaining the work they have to do now. First she reviews work they have obviously talked about before.

T: 'Hands up those who were drawing long things on Wednesday.'

They tell her what they drew.

Various children: 'A crocodile, a blackboard, the Minster.'

There followed a discussion of long buildings, spires and square towers.

T: 'Right, so somebody is going to draw long things today, talk about your ideas together.

You're going to take a boundary and a tray of things between you and do some partitions.'

(Now group of 4, 2b 2g)

Karen gets two trays and a boundary, which is a wipe clean board with a boundary drawn on it. Two trays of Unifix cubes.

Child: 'What do we have to do?'

Karen: 'Make partitions.'

Karen puts five white cubes on one side and three black on the side of the board and draws a line down the middle.

Karen: 'Mine's finished.'

Child: 'Partitions isn't it Karen?'

Karen: 'Yes, partitions.'

The other children do the same. Karen, who has finished, draws the line thicker.

Karen: 'I'm waiting for you' (to teacher).

The teacher comes to talk to the other girl first, then Karen.

T: 'Tell me about your set, what did you have?'

Karen: 'A set of black and a set of white.'

T: 'What did you have to start with?'

Karen: 'A set of blocks. A boundary.'

The teacher re-arranged her blocks, rubbing out the line.

T: 'I'll try to trick you. Don't move them.'

Karen giggles and draws a line.

T: 'Why did you get two lines in all round there?'

Karen: 'That's the circle that gets the whites in.'

T: 'Rub out that one because you've gone all round and that's a boundary. Show me what you did – Yes, that partitioned off the black and the white, so you didn't need that line, did you?'

The teacher re-arranges the line again. Karen gets it right. A boy is allowed to get a wet towel, for them so they can rub out their own lines and re-arrange their cubes themselves.

Karen does one more. This is easy. (She gets it right.)

Me: 'What's the line you've drawn called?'

Karen: 'A sub-set.'

Me: 'No, the *line*.'

Karen: 'A boundary.'

Me: 'What's the *yellow* line you're drawing?'

Karen: 'A pen.'

Karen's last cubes were arranged in a very different way (by herself she couldn't do it).

12.00 Time to go home.

Interview with child

Activity 1/2 Choosing a book was an easy and enjoyable activity for Karen, and was a familiar routine, unlike the demand to draw and write. She is able to draw and copy writing but was again unable, in the interview, to read the words.

Activity 3 Karen found this easy, familiar and enjoyable and was highly involved in the work. She demonstrated her understanding of some of the mathematical concepts – bigger, most etc.

Activity 4 Karen was again fully involved in a familiar task. In the main she practised ideas previously experienced, and showed herself adept at basic partitioning, although still confused about boundaries and partitions.

Interview with teacher

Did the child get out of this activity what you expected?

Activity 1 / 2 Yes, she had chosen the book for a good reason.

Activity 3 She was able to say they were the same length – she matched them.

Activity 4 Yes she had it clearer altogether. She did put the boundary right round, but she had a good reason ie 'There's a space there.'

Was the activity a success / failure? and why?

Activity 1 / 2 Yes, it made them think and look at the book.

Activity 3 Yes, showed evidence of maths input.

Activity 4 Yes, good practice. Had a clear idea of what she was doing.

In the light of this what will you do next?

Activity 1 / 2 They choose library books every week. Writing will not be repeated for six weeks. We talk about the books when they come back. I will exhibit the books they made in the book corner.

Activity 3 She's getting the idea of equivalent and non-equivalent sets – we will build on that.

Activity 4 It's something that needs re-inforcing all the time. She needs more practice in other ways.

Guidelines for discussion

1   Examine Karen's play experiences in this session. Which areas of the curriculum did the play encompass? Comment on the role and quality of adult intervention.

2 What did Karen gain, socially and academically, from each activity? Do you believe the activities to have been appropriate to Karen's capabilities?

3 i) This teacher has 33 children in the class. The age range is 4.10 to 5.4. She has no adult help during this session. Examine the strengths and weaknesses of the session with these facts in mind.

   ii) Which factors have the most influence on the positive aspects of the session?

4 The reading activity was apparently enjoyed by Karen and handled sensitively by the teacher. However, when the observer asked Karen to read to her the child replied by pointing out she had done her reading today! Are there any implications of such a comment? (The interchange between observer and child is not reproduced in this text.)

Kevin

The school which Kevin attends is in a very mixed environment in the centre of a small town. The catchment area is large and encompasses the very affluent to the socially deprived. Kevin is in his second term in a class of 38 children. The age range is 4+ to 5.8. The arrangement of the classroom provides plenty of space. It is well equipped and everything is easily accessible to the children. There are tables and chairs to accommodate two groups of children at a time. The activity areas are well separated and clearly defined. All the equipment is fully utilised.

The teacher has regular parental help and she has auxiliary assistance for two sessions per week. She has a gentle sense of fun and is popular with the children. Her sessions are well organised and the children are responsive and orderly. The teacher describes Kevin as being a little self-conscious and lacking in confidence. However, she feels that he has settled well and is making good progress in all areas.

Teacher's intentions for Kevin, with her activity descriptions, reasons and expectations.

Activity 1

Description	– *Number* – length
Reasons	– Topic on length started at the beginning of the week. Done basic sorting of long and short. Now going one step further – longer than. Use of Unifix cubes to make rods – compare them. Link to collection of long things on the wall. They have made models of long things
Expectations	– Sorting, counting, talk of more and less. Use longer than

Activity 2

Description	– *Making sweets*
Reasons	– Made a basket yesterday. Today we are going to make sweets to go

inside it. They will take it home for Valentine's Day and give it to someone they love. They are going to decide who themselves

Expectations – Language development from discussion. Counting experience, social development through sharing. I have asked the parent helper to talk about 'powdery', 'cream', 'stiff'; to have them roll butter not too big or too small, use of finger tips, rolling lightly and gently

Activity 3

Description – *Story*
Reason – Good finish to day
Expectations – Language enjoyment

Activity log

Activity 1 (5, 1b 4g; 4.11–5.5; teacher-chosen)

Register. Assembly.

9.25   All together with teacher in the carpeted corner area. They do the weather chart.

T: 'Yesterday we made some baskets, today we are going to make some sweets to go in them and tomorrow you can take them home.'

She explains about St Valentine's Day, ... who they are going to give the sweets to ... 'someone you love. ...'

She gives a general explanation of the work to be done today, some are going to do cooking, some sorting, all will have some free choice time, some will be sorting long hair from short hair. This last is a craft activity and she explains how to do it.

T: (Naming group of six children) 'are to do cooking, go to the welfare assistant and she will tell you what to do.'

One other group is to work with the parent, one to stay with her (the teacher) and one group can have free time. She tells them they can play with the sand, water, paint and the Wendy House.

Kevin's group remain on the carpet with the teacher. She gives each child a straw.

T: 'What can you tell me about these straws?'

Kevin: 'Some are short and some are long.'

Others say: 'Bendy, twisty ... a hole ... you can look through ... blow through.'

T: 'How could we sort them out?'

A child: 'Small and big.'

Kevin: 'We could put ... I don't know.'

The children have various suggestions.

Child: 'Big – it's long.'

T: 'What's a better word for that?'

Kevin: 'Long.'

The teacher puts two circles on the floor with labels saying *long* and *short*. The children have to take a straw and decide if it is long or short. They suggest closing their eyes, the teacher agrees. They do this, then they put the straws in the circles and discuss if they are right.

Kevin puts his in the *long* circle.

T: 'What can you tell me about these . . .?'

Kevin: 'That one (long set) has more in it. . . . That one has three that one has two.'

They all discuss this.

Kevin: 'There's one more.'

T: 'How can we find out who's right? . . . Let's put them together and match them.'

They do and find out which set has more in. (They have matched one straw from each set.)

The teacher gives each child a straw and asks him to make a rod of Unifix that is longer than the straw.

Kevin measures his rod (half made) against his long straw.

T: 'Kevin, which one is longer?'

He points to the rod. The teacher puts the straw on the other side of the rod.

T: 'Is the rod still longer?'

Kevin nods.

Whilst this is going on, one or two children come to show the teacher a painting or craft work. She makes an interested comment or question about each item.

They put all the Unifix rods together and discuss which is the longest. (They were asked to make a rod longer than their straw.)

T: 'How can we tell? Put it together, is it longer?'

Child: 'Put it to the bottom.'

Kevin seems interested. He does all that he is asked and watches the discussions with the other children.

10.00 They move to a table with pencils, crayons – rather old ones. The teacher sits with them.

They each have worksheets.

T: 'I've drawn a worm and I want you to draw a longer worm.

I've drawn a scarf and I want you to draw a longer scarf.

What do you have to put on the top?'

Child: 'Your name.'

T: 'Yes, you don't have to do any of the writing.'

Kevin writes his name on the line at the top.

Kevin: 'The line is longer than my name!'

T: 'Yes, so it is!'

Kevin draws a worm that is the same size as the one already drawn, then he hears a girl say: 'It's longer'. He looks back at his and realises he has made it the same length, so he rubs out the end and draws it longer.

He draws a scarf that is short and shows it to the teacher.

T: 'Tell me about the worm? ... is the scarf longer?'

Kevin: 'Well ... No.'

T: 'What will you have to do?'

Kevin: 'I think I'll have to draw some more.'

T: 'Do what you have to do.'

Kevin rubs out the scarf and draws it longer. He shows it to the teacher who asks him questions about it. He replies.

Kevin: 'It was too short ... I drew it longer.'

10.10 He starts to colour it in, does the teacher's worm too and sharpens his pencil. The sharpener is available on the table.

10.12 T: (to all) 'Would the pink group go to Mrs Helper, please?'

Kevin fetches the model he made yesterday, he told me about it.

Kevin: 'A spaceship, these are guns at the front ... engines.'

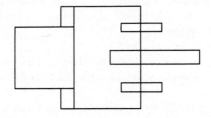

(cardboard boxes)

Kevin: 'We had to put something long on, this is a long gun.'

He takes it to the teacher and they talk about controls, where it would go, how many men could go in, making a door.

T: 'Are you going to paint it?'

Kevin: 'I'm going to paint it black so they won't see what it is.'

Teacher asks about lights, then says he can paint it this afternoon.

Kevin goes to the Unifix on the carpet and fixes some together.

10.20 Snacks

10.30 Playtime

Activity 2 (5, 1b 3g; 4.11–5.5; teacher-chosen)

T: 'If you are a blue person and were working with me before play, please stand

up. You are going to work with Mrs X' (Welfare assistant – WA)
(Teacher had written instructions and equipment prepared for WA, which the latter carefully followed.)
WA gives instructions about washing, scrubbing, drying hands, germs, etc. They go and wash their hands and put aprons on. WA washes her hands too.
WA: 'What is this, how would it feel?' (Margarine)
Children: 'Gooey and squeezy, it would slip through your fingers.'
WA talks about the chocolate being a powder, then asks Kevin about the chocolate strands.
Kevin: 'I've forgotten the name.'
WA mentions icing sugar.
Kevin: 'She (Mummy) mixes it for cakes. I don't know what she does for sweeties with.'
The WA continues introducing the ingredients, what they are like; one soft, one powder, one in pieces. She puts the margarine in bowls and the children take turns to stir it with a long wooden spoon.
Kevin: 'It's stiff.'
He stirs it for a short time. They talked about the colour – yellow, and what will happen when they add the chocolate to the margarine.
Children: 'A different taste . . . sweet . . . sour . . . creamy . . . a different colour.'
Kevin: 'It will be a yellowy brown.'
Children: 'It smells toffee!'
Kevin: 'It smells like chocolate.'
WA: 'What's happened to the margarine? . . . hard, soft, stiff . . .'
Kevin: 'It's even tighter now.' (He is trying to mix it.)
Kevin is otherwise quiet, he does what he is asked. He looks at what he is doing.
WA: 'It's gone into lumps. It's a bit hard.'
Child: 'It's a bit stiff.'
WA: 'We've got to get rid of all the white.'
Kevin licked his fingers and was sent to wash his hands, the WA said she forgets sometimes and licks her fingers.
WA finishes stirring the mixture for the children.
Kevin: 'It's not white yet . . . lighty brown.'
Child: 'Like dog's food.'
WA: 'It will go hard, not hard like rock.'
Kevin: 'I suppose we're going to use those brown things next (chocolate strands.'
WA: 'Once hard, get it in your fingers, make it into a ball. Very gently, then drop it into the chocolate strands. It gets wet and sticky.'
Kevin had a little difficulty rolling the mixture with the fingertips of one hand. He dropped the ball into the plate of chocolate. The WA rolled it around and put it on a plate to dry.
Kevin: 'What do I do now?'

WA: 'Another one.'
The next one was better.
Kevin: 'This feels comfortable.... This is going hard.'
WA: 'Yes, they will go hard, eventually.'
WA: 'You can lick your fingers now.'
Kevin puts his fingers in his mouth.
WA: 'Not you!'
He hadn't finished, she meant the other three.
He shared the mixing bowl with a girl, neither took any notice of the other, but took turns when the adult told them to.
He finished and licked his fingers, washed the bowls and dried them.

11.45 Finished altogether, he sits on the carpet with the teacher.

Activity 3 (Whole class: teacher-chosen)

All sitting on the carpet by the teacher, except four finishing painting models with the parent. Kevin listens, looking at the teacher. The story is from a book of collected stories. The teacher reads from the book; there are no pictures for the child to see.
'Three wishes.'
Kevin, sitting at the side of the teacher's knee, listens well. They have a song about 'Driving in our car.'

Interviews with child

Activity 1 Kevin enjoyed the session and knew what to do. He had difficulty in telling the teacher how to sort the straws out but it became clear that he was able to sort the sets once he knew what the attributes were. Similarly, although he made mistakes in the drawing activity he understood, by the end of the activity, the concept of 'long' and 'longer than'.

Activity 2 He found this an easy, but enjoyable activity and was able to demonstrate his understanding of it during the interview.

Activity 3 He was able to tell the story in the correct order.

Interview with teacher

Did the child get out of this activity what you expected?

Activity 1 Yes, he'd remembered what we'd done the day before and could put straws into sets. He made his Unifix rod longer and put the ends together correctly. He made a mistake but corrected it himself, showing that he understood it.

Activity 2 He knew he had made chocolate truffles, and what they were made with. He knew about the equipment he had used, and that the mixture was loose and then it was stiff.

Was it a success/failure? Why?

Activity 1 Success. Completed the task with understanding.

Activity 2 Success, for same reasons.

In the light of this what will you do next?

Activity 1 Sorting sets. So far we have used knitting needles and straws ie rigid. We will now use wool and string – flexible. I will ask him to find two or three things longer than a paintbrush. I hope to link it to number and do an investigation.

Activity 2 We'll talk about what we did – ingredients, recipe, sequence. Share truffles out, put them into baskets (cutting and folding exercises). Talk about who they are going to give them to.

Guidelines for discussion

1 What can we learn from this teacher's use of adult helpers?

2 The quality of adult intervention is very important. What are your comments regarding the child/adult dialogue in this session with particular reference to the teacher's description of the child and his needs?

3 What are your observations about the teacher's intentions for the session, her awareness of the child's response to the activities, and her future plans?

4 What do you think Kevin gained, socially and intellectually, from this session?

Mandy

Mandy attends part-time at a school which was built in the early 1950s and is situated in a council estate on the fringe of a large town. It is a rather socially deprived area with a high level of unemployment. There are 27 children in the class, eight of whom attend mornings only. The age range is 4.6 to 5.5

The classroom is quite large but affords little space because of the number of tables and chairs. Ample storage space is provided by built-in cupboards – with formica worktops which are piled with un-finished models, puzzles, maths apparatus, paper, children's paintings, etc. There is a home corner, carpeted area, and a folding bookcase which is permanently closed! The room is very cluttered, a shared lobby area outside the room has sand and water trays and a small cooker. The teacher has a kindly manner, but she is rather tense and speaks very loudly. Fifteen hours a week ancillary assistance is provided for a child with special needs. There is an auxiliary for five hours a week but no parent helpers.

The teacher describes Mandy as being calm and attentive. She has presented no problems.

Teacher's intentions for Mandy, with her activity descriptions, reasons and expectations.

Activity 1

Description	– *Looking at Houses book*
Reasons	– Pre-reading activity
Expectations	– Reinforce work on 'families'. Make links between family and house roof colour (*123 Away* scheme)

Activity 2

Description	– *Cooking* – house shaped biscuits
Reasons	– Science activity
Expectations	– A lot of fun

Activity 3

Description	– *Making a stand up house*
Reasons	– Pre-reading activity; art and craft
Expectations	– Fine motor skills and enjoyment

Activity 4

Description	– *Reading* – flash cards
Reasons	– Pre-reading activity
Expectations	– Associate words with what child has been doing

Activity 5 and 6

Planned activities on building, with bricks and sand, but these did not happen.

Activity log

Activity 1 (20, 10b 10g; 4.5–5.5; teacher-chosen)

10.00 Children have just returned from Assembly.

T: 'Come and sit with me and we'll talk about what you have been doing.'
They sit with teacher on carpeted area. Children offer various 'news items' to the general discussion. Mandy takes no active part but is listening with interest. Teacher then shows them a supplementary book from *123 Away* – on 'Houses'. Children are asked to volunteer the correct colours involved.
Teacher then tells Mandy's group that they are going to make a biscuit in the shape of a house and that Mrs X (Auxiliary) will help them.

Activity 2 (4, 1b 3g; 4+; teacher-chosen)

10.10 Aux tells children that they are going to make a biscuit in the shape of a house. Shows them the cutters and ingredients.
Aux asks group which is margarine, sugar, flour. (These ingredients are all in appropriate packaging.)
Aux then weighs ingredients while group watch.
Aux suggests they take it in turns to stir.
They are invited to choose the colour for their 'biscuit house'. Mandy chooses blue.

10.20 There is a lot of conversation going on with the Auxiliary.
Aux: 'Why do we break eggs? How do we break them?'
Aux: 'Who helps Mummy to cook at home?'
Two children say they do (not Mandy).
Aux divides the dough so that they all have a basin containing an equal share. (They are wearing aprons with velcro fastenings. Most of them are not fastened and the aprons keep falling down their arms. Aux has made no attempt to rectify this.)
Aux then adds the chosen colour to the respective bowls.
Aux to Mandy: 'You are making a lovely blue bowl but not very blue biscuits.'
Mandy continues to stir it with a wooden spoon but there is little improvement.
Aux to Mandy: 'Take it in your hands and play with it like playdough then the colour will get into it.'
Mandy to Aux: 'I choosed the colour didn't I?'
Group are all very absorbed. They are obviously enjoying it and there is plenty of conversation about what they are doing.
Mandy is the first to roll out her dough.
She tries to cut it with the cutter the wrong way up! The cutter is a template of a house shape.
Aux points out her mistake and this time Mandy gets it right.
Aux: 'Your colour reminds me of another one. Do you think so?'
Mandy does not respond.
Aux: 'Oh well, as long as you think it looks blue!' (it looks more like green!)

10.40 Mandy now makes a second house.

Aux: 'Now you can play with the dough you have left. You really don't need it.'

Aux takes group and the tray of biscuits over to cooker in corner of room. She is very careful to ensure that group are not too near it.

10.50   Childen are told it is indoor playtime and when they have washed their hands and taken off their aprons they can choose puzzles or plasticine to play with.

Activity unplanned (4, 1b 3g; 4+; teacher-chosen)

11.00   Towards the end of playtime T sat with Mandy's group and asked them to lay a table with some toy crockery and cutlery she has (cups, saucers, plates, knives, forks and spoons).

T to Mandy: 'Are there enough cups for everyone?'

Mandy puts some more cups on some more saucers – there are now more than enough for everyone!

T asks Mandy to count how many people there are.

Mandy counts five – correctly as she has included the teacher.

T asks her then to lay the table for them all and the others watch.

Mandy puts out the correct number of items but gets knives and forks on wrong side of plates.

There has been no conversation at all from the children during this playtime 'interlude'.

Activity unplanned (20, 10b 10g; 4.5–5.5; teacher-chosen)

11.10   Children sit outside classroom in shared area where television is kept. The children are sitting on a small carpet 'sample' each.

Most children are watching a TV programme with interest although a few are restless (programme features the king and queen – who this time encounter a dragon who cannot sleep)!

Two auxiliaries are in the classroom clearing up after indoor playtime. The main story in programme finishes and children become increasingly restless and there is a fair amount of conversation.

T: 'I hope you are watching.'

Programme ends. Teacher tells children to go back into classroom and sit on carpet because she wants to have a little conversation about day and night.

Activity unplanned (20, 10b, 4.5–5.5; teacher-chosen)

11.17   Whole class with teacher – on carpet.

T tells children that Sally has been having nightmares because she is afraid of the dark. Children are asked if they are afraid of the dark like Sally?

Children volunteer this and a variety of other fears.

Small group conversations begin amongst the children.
Teacher asks them to talk to whole class not just the children next to them.
T asks how many children have a little light left on in their bedrooms at night. Most say they do.
The general conversations continue and the class is very noisy and restless.
Teacher intersperses her dialogue with class with remonstrations re the 'break away' group discussions which are taking place – but they do not stop!
Conversation ranges to what time children go to bed.
T: 'Give Sally some tips as to what she can do to help her get over her problem of being frightened in the dark.'
Children suggest:
'Teddy in bed.'
'Cover head with the sheet.'
General conversation goes into their own fears again and more small group conversations arise. The class are very restless.

11.25 Teacher now tells Mandy's cooking group to go to auxiliary to find out what has happened to their biscuits.

Activity 2 (continued)

Aux shows children cooked biscuits.
Aux: 'Would you like to have a taste?'
They all say they would.
Aux breaks up blue house first. They all have a piece.
Aux: 'Does it taste blue?'
Mandy: 'No let's have yellow now.'
Aux breaks up yellow biscuit and hands it round. 'Does it taste different?'
Children: 'Yes.'
Aux: 'How different? What does it taste like?'
No response.
Aux looks at crumbs left in box and says: 'Oh crumbs!'
There is no response from group.
Aux: 'Now we are going to do something else.'

Activity 3 (4; 1b 3g; 4+; teacher-chosen)

11.30 Aux: 'Now we are going to make a house from card.'
Aux has made a sample house for them. She tells them it can be their own house like hers, or from *123 Away*.
The cards are folded so that when the houses are cut they will have a back and front (see diagram below).
(Aux's example for children)

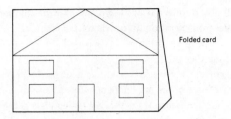

Folded card

Children start to draw and colour their houses.

11.35   Mandy is busy colouring hers.

Aux sits with them and colours her house at the same time.

Mandy: 'I've got a garage.'

Aux: 'So have I but you can't see mine because it isn't joined on to the house – is yours?'

Mandy: 'Yes.' She continues to colour in.

Class still incredibly noisy. Teacher's voice dominates and therefore the conversations taking place amongst children rise to match it.

Mandy has tried several coloured felt tipped pens none of which work! She has a struggle to fill in the windows. She gives up.

Teacher says someone is making an awful noise.

Mandy starts to cut out her house under the watchful eye of the Aux. However, she is not watchful enough and as her attention is momentarily focused on another child Mandy cuts across the fold!

Another child in the group is busily doing the same!

Aux has not noticed what either of them have done although she is talking to them.

Aux suddenly notices what Mandy has done. 'Do you know what you have done?'

She then notices the other child: 'You've done the same.'

Aux: 'Oh well, I suppose it is my fault. I should have watched you more carefully.'

Mandy appears quite unconcerned and turns her house over and starts to draw the 'back'. Aux returns to table with sellotape and takes the house from Mandy and sticks along where the fold had been.

Mandy abandons her colouring of back of house and decides to write her name on it instead. She had collected her 'name card' from her 'work' box.

She writes in very inadequate felt pen –

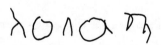

She has her name upside down.

The group have all virtually finished their houses now. Aux tells them they are going to do the 'flash cards' from *123 Away*.

Activity 4 (4, 1b 3g; 4+; teacher-chosen)

There are four cards – yellow, hat, blue, red.
Aux then starts to read from supplementary reader used earlier by teacher – about houses.
Aux asks group where she should begin reading on page?
They tell her – with mixed success.
She starts to read. (The noise is so great that I cannot hear her although I am positioned very close to group.)

11.55 Aux tells children to go and get something to play with because it is too noisy for them to hear her.
Just as children are about to go Teacher arrives and asks to see their houses.
Group collect them from worktop at side of room. Teacher has a perfunctory glance and moves away without commenting. Teacher and auxiliary do not communicate in any way.
T shouts to class to get their coats on ready to go home or to go to dinner. Dinner lady appears and helps vocally with this exercise!

12.00 Children leave room.

Interviews with child

Activity 1 Mandy was interested in, and enjoyed this activity despite the fact that she took no active part. In the interview she demonstrated understanding of the content.

Activity 2 Mandy was able to explain what was made and the necessary ingredients. She also said that she had done the activity before, when making buns.

Activity 3 'I drawed a house and cut it wrong, and the pens wouldn't work' was Mandy's perception of this activity. She does not understand the principle of leaving the fold.

Activity 4 No interview. Child left in the ensuing confusion.

Interview with teacher

Did the child get out of this activity what you expected?

1 Would have been better as a small group activity.
2 I didn't see the activity. She knew which was hers.

3 I didn't see it.

4 I don't know. I was doing something else.

a) Was it a success/failure   b) Why?

1 Success – she did take part. It could have been better.

2 Success – she enjoyed it and was talking about it.

3 Success – she was interested in what she was doing.

4 I didn't see it.

In the light of this what will you do next?

1 Work with same idea with a small group.

2 Perhaps different shape and flavour.

3 Probably make 3-dimensional houses.

4 More flash cards connected with the reading scheme.

Guidelines for discussion

1   Discuss the overall organisation and balance of the session.

2   Evaluate the appropriateness of each activity with reference to its:
     a) presentation, including materials
     b) adult help
     c) match of task to child

3   If the teacher asked for your constructive criticism regarding each activity how would you reply? Using the information available, and retaining the same curriculum areas and expectations as stated by the teacher – which activities would you re-plan with her? – and how?

4   Was noise a problem in this session? If so, could you suggest alternative ways of organising the classroom which might overcome it?

5   What assessment or diagnosis of children's work did the teacher carry out?

Roger

Roger is in his first term at a small rural primary school which is housed in an old building. He is one of a group of three under-fives who attend for three afternoons a week. The school, which has only two classes, is situated in a fairly isolated farming community. There are 14 children in Roger's class and the age range is from 4.6 to 7 years. There is auxiliary provision for five hours a week, but no parental help. There is no play group in the area.

The classroom, although fairly small, is attractively arranged and there is ample space for the number of children it accommodates. There is a home corner, shop, sand, water, a book corner, and carpeted area. Room-divider shelving serves the dual purpose of providing adequate storage space and creating clearly defined activity areas. The teacher is warm, lively, interesting, artistic, and has an excellent rapport with the children. The ambiance of her classroom reflects these characteristics. The school has a secure 'family' atmosphere – perhaps unsurprising as indeed, many of the children are actually related!

The teacher describes Roger as being an extremely shy child. However, she feels he has grown in confidence in the short time that he has been at school. He has an older brother in the class which helps to give him security.

Teacher's intentions for Roger, with her activity descriptions, reasons and expectations.

Activity 1

Description – *Senses* – 'feely' box

Activity 2

Description – *Covering 'feely' box*

Activity 3

Description – *Choice*

Activity 4

Description – *TV Programme* – words and pictures

Activity 5

Description – *Choice* (continuation of Activity 3)

The teacher had the same overall reasons for all of these activities ie to achieve fine motor skills, and socialisation with peer group, listening/responding to others, and language development. Her expectations for all the activities were for experience and enjoyment.

Activity log

Activity 1 (All class (14), 10b 4g; 4+–7+; teacher-chosen)

1.20   Children gathered round teacher on carpet. Teacher has a 'feely' box which is at present empty.

Teacher discusses senses. She asks children to close their eyes and then moves very quietly round the room and they have to point to where she is. Roger is joining in with enthusiasm. He points accurately. Teacher sits down again and asks for some suggestions as to what would be interesting things to put in the box. He offers a fir cone as a good idea. Teacher agrees and Roger looks pleased. He grins at the boy sitting next to him and appears very comfortable in the group.

Roger is showing signs of restlessness. His interest in the feely box has waned. He turns to the boy next to him and starts to chat. Teacher now asks for volunteers to find an object for the feely box. Roger immediately shows renewed interest and kneels up in his enthusiasm to be chosen. He isn't. The children who are chosen are all full time and it is arranged that they will put one thing each into the box during the afternoon when no-one is looking. Then children will be able to have turns at guessing.

Teacher mentions that they are to cover the real feely box which they will keep. Asks for volunteers. All three part time children put up their hands and are chosen.

1.35   Teacher tells the three children to go to the table where the auxiliary is waiting for them.

Activity 2 (3 (all p/t) 2b 1g; 4+; teacher-chosen)

Auxiliary tells them they are going to cover the 'feely' box to make it look attractive.

Roger picks up a piece of polyester filling (for quilting) and says it feels like a sheep. (This is a rural community and most of the farms have sheep.)

Auxiliary smiles and agrees. She asks other boy if they have had any more lambs this week.

Boy: 'Yes, two, they've both got the same mummy.'

Aux: 'What do we call them then?'

Boy: 'Twins.'

Roger: 'I know what it is if there's three – driblets.'

Auxiliary smiles at him. 'Good boy. Yes we call them triplets don't we?'

Roger shows no sign of having noticed the correction.

Roger sticks two pieces of polyester onto the box. The pva sticks to his hands as he has applied it very liberally. He sits for several minutes totally absorbed with opening and closing his fingers and watching the effect. He then discovers by rolling it with his finger and thumb he can start to get it off his hands. He loses interest now and picks up more polyester. (While he was playing with the glue there was no interaction at all between Roger and the others who were chatting to the Auxiliary while they worked. The Auxiliary glanced at him several times but didn't intervene.)

Roger to Auxiliary: 'I'm going to make balls with this.' Teases out the

polyester and starts to roll it into irregular lumps.
He sticks lumps to the box and says he's finished.

1.50 Auxiliary tells him to wash his hands, take his apron off, and choose something else.

Activity 3 (Individual; 4+; child-chosen)

1.55 Chooses plasticine table on which there are plasticine boards, pastry cutters, cutter wheel etc. He forces pieces into pastry cutter shapes and then pushes them through the other side. He is sitting on his own and is totally engrossed.

2.00 Teacher calls children over to watch TV programme: *Words and Pictures.*

Activity 4 (Whole class; 4+–7+; teacher-chosen)

Roger sits with the others. He is watching intently – as are the other children. Teacher has given them each a piece of material or garment. Roger joins in with forming letter L shape in the air. Children now pretend to do the washing as on programme, using their material. Roger doesn't attempt to 'dress' in his as the other children do. He sits watching the programme.

2.17 Programme ends. Teacher asks the children to think of some words beginning with 'L'. The f/t children start to put up their hands immediately. Teacher asks them in turn. Roger sits listening and watching but doesn't take an active part. (Neither do the other two p/t children.) He listens intently as teacher says that 'l' is like a 1 (one) and a bigger i without the dot. They all form shape in the air.

Activity 1 (contd)

All class with teacher.

Teacher asks if the children chosen have put things in the 'feely box' yet. They have and hand her the box. She starts to choose children to feel an object inside and guess what it is. Teacher points out that they will have to ask children concerned if they have guessed correctly because she doesn't know what is in the box either. Children obviously enjoy this.
Roger has a turn to feel and says he can feel a dog. Teacher elicits from him that it is a toy dog and not a real one. Children all laugh (including Roger). He says he can feel a paint brush as well. Teacher says she hopes it isn't a wet painty one. More laughter.

2.30 The activity continues and is obviously being enjoyed and there is full participation by the group. Teacher then says it is time to go out to play.

Activity 3 (condt)

As soon as Roger came in from play he went straight over to the plasticine. He is filling the pastry cutters with plasticine again. He is very absorbed in what he is doing but every now and then he looks up and gazes round the room at the other children. He seems quite contented on his own. He makes no attempt to make contact with the other children. He and his brother exchange a grin across the room. A boy pauses as he passes Roger's table and asks him what he's making.

Roger: 'These.' Points to four moulds of plasticine which he has on the table. Boy nods and grins and walks off. Roger makes some more. He has stopped pushing the plasticine through now. Having carefully flattened it he is leaving it in the pastry cutter.

He stops playing and is gazing at two boys across the room who are building something with 'build and play' construction set.

Roger is still watching the boys. His chin is cupped in his hands and he looks totally absorbed. Roger gets up and wanders over to the boys. Roger stands watching the boys.

One boy looks at him and smiles.

Roger: 'What are you making?'

Boy: ' A tower and it's going to have a bridge.'

Roger sits at their table and watches them.

Other boy to Roger: 'D'you want to do these for me?' Holds up a six flat oblong.

Roger nods eagerly. Beside the table is a large cardboard box half full of flats of different sizes (see diagram below) and screws.

Roger very meticulously sorts through the box and correctly collects the oblongs.

There is no conversation. All three boys are absorbed in their own parts of the activity.

Boy to Roger: 'That's enough now I think.' Roger has collected about 30 pieces.

Roger sits down again and watches.

Boy to Roger: 'I need lots of screws.'

Roger gets up immediately and starts to get screws and nuts from the box.

Boy: 'That's enough now. Thanks.' Roger sits down again looking very pleased. He watches quietly.

Other boy to Roger: 'D'you want to help make it?' Roger looks delighted and nods vigorously.

Two older boys exchange glances and both nod. Boy to Roger: 'You can screw these in twos if you want.' Points to oblongs.

Roger frowns and hesitates.

Boy: 'D'you know what to do?'

Roger shakes his head.

Boy shows him (see diagram). Roger starts confidently and correctly carries out task.

Roger is totally absorbed in joining oblongs.

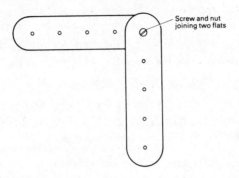

Screw and nut joining two flats

Roger's task as set by 7 year olds

3.07   T: 'You have a few minutes left, children, before you pack up.'
Teacher comes over to Roger's table and asks what they are making. They tell her. She asks Roger if he has enjoyed the afternoon. He says yes and smiles at her. Teacher tells boy that they can put the model on the window ledge so that they can continue with it tomorrow.

3.10   Teacher tells children to pack away what they have been using. She asks Roger if he will please put the plasticine away as she thinks he has been the only one playing with it this afternoon. She asks if he knows where it goes. He says he does and puts it away.

Teacher tells class to get their coats and come back and line up as quickly as possible because they are a bit late. She says 'good afternoon' to them and the auxiliary escorts them outside.

Interviews with child

Activity 1 & 2 Roger enjoyed the session and understood the requirements. However he lacked the appropriate motor skills to apply the glue with precision.

Activity 3 Activity 3 turned from a free choice of plasticine to a task dictated by older children. He was able to follow the instructions and carry out the necessary operations. He was able, in his interview, to describe his actions and understandings accurately.

Activity 4 Was able to recount the essence of the TV programme, and knew that the letter 'l' was involved.

Interview with teacher

Did the child get out of this activity what you expected?

Activity 1 I was pleased to see him chatting to the boy next to him.

Activity 2 I didn't see what he did but I chatted with the auxiliary after and she said he joined in with a conversation and seemed to enjoy the activity. She mentioned he appeared fascinated by the pva.

Activity 3 Didn't notice him much but when I did he seemed absorbed with making moulds. And in the continuation activity was pleased that he was apparently accepted very well by the older boys. Shows he is part of the class.

Activity 4 Took part very well.

Was it a success or a failure? Why?

Activity 1 & 2 Success I think. He joined in and seemed to enjoy both activities.

Activity 3 Seemed successful. He joined in of his own accord.

Activity 4 Yes. He was an active participant, which represented progress.

In the light of this what will you do next?

Activity 1 & 2 More of similar activities.

Activity 3 More of similar activities. I will ask older boys if they would wait to continue on Wednesday so that he can join in. I won't force them to do so however, as that would not be fair to them.

Activity 4 More of similar activities.

Guidelines for discussion

1   The teacher has two overall aims for the under-fives in her class. Have these aims been fulfilled in this session? How?

2   With particular reference to the teacher's description of Roger, examine the appropriateness of the afternoon's experience.

3   List evidence of 'teacher awareness' from the information in the log of session. Also examine this aspect with reference to the teacher's intentions, her post-session comments and her future intentions.

4 Comment on the quality of the adult intervention during the session.

5 Play is considered to be central to the learning process of young children. Comment on the quality of Roger's play experience.

Ryan

The school Ryan attends is large, modern, and situated in an area of high employment and comparative affluence. All the children in his class are four year olds who attend part-time. There are 14 children in each session.

The classroom is light, spacious, and attractive. There is a wide range of good quality and easily accessible equipment. The room is colourful and well-ordered. The teacher is kind, lively, and has an excellent rapport with the children. Her sessions are well-prepared. There is always at least one parent helper and the class also has part-time auxiliary provision.

The teacher describes Ryan as being an immature, shy child who needs to learn to play and interact with his peers.

Teacher's intentions for Ryan in this session, with her activity description, reasons and expectations.

Activity 1

Description — *Class discussion* with teacher
Reasons — His speech is immature, vocabulary limited, sentence construction poor. Opportunity to speak before peer group and confidence to do so. (Did not volunteer speech last term.) To aid 'Listening skills'. Increase knowledge
Expectations — Vocabularly extension. General knowledge. Finding out more about peers. Offering information about self. Putting ideas and thought into a logical order to relate. Help with sentence construction. Extension of maths concepts

Activity 2

Description — *Colouring in circles*
Reasons — Shape recognition and naming
Expectations — Extension of maths concepts, naming properties

Activity 3

Description — *Painting* speckles on his clay frog

Reasons	– Completing models of a frog prior to taking it home – part of frog topic. Observational and manipulative skills
Expectations	– Satisfaction of completing a task

Activity 4

Description	– *Cutting out pictures* – from magazines – what belongs to Mummy. Matching 'many' to 'one'
Reasons	– Pre-maths activity. Manipulative skills
Expectations	– Number conservation – matching 3 to 1. Manipulation, hand-eye coordination

Activity 5

Description	– *Singing*. All children with teacher
Reasons	– Reinforcement of left-right concept
Expectations	– Ability to tell left from right

An additional expectation of all the activities was that they should be fun.

Activity log

Activity 1 (Group – 12 children, 7b, 5g Age – 4+; teacher-chosen activity)

1.30   Children arrive in school and sit round teacher on carpet. Two children have brought pictures drawn by children at home. (They have used felt tipped pens and powder paint respectively.)
A discussion begins about eggs – painting eggs – 'what do we do with eggs – what is an oval shape?' All sit making an oval shape (including teacher.) T chooses three children to show class how they can sit in an oval shape. It is agreed the shapes look more like circles. They decide they have to make the sides longer to achieve an oval.

Registration. All count 12 children and 4 adults (including me!) T says this is a set of 12 and a set of 4. Asks how many altogether?
Child volunteers 16 after a very short pause.
Children on carpet with teacher.
T asks a child to bring a shape card over from the box. He brings a rectangle. T asks children the name of the shape and they tell her correctly (difficult to ascertain how many are responding with the correct answer – Ryan is certainly not one of them!)
Children take turns to collect a shape card from the box. Cards are named in turn; edges are counted; straight or curved discussed; difference between square and rectangle. Shapes include – hexagon, diamond, oval, circle, irregular.

1.55   Ryan suddenly 'comes to life' and asks if he can get the next one.

T says yes and then forgets and chooses someone else.

Ryan calls out in protest 'You said I could do it!'

T: 'I'm sorry I did and then I forgot. Remind me when we have looked at this one.'

He doesn't have to as she remembers. He walks over to the box and chooses an irregular shape – which he fails to name correctly.

2.00   T then tells the children which activities they are going to do and explains where they go to start the first one.

Activity 2 (2, 2b; 4+; teacher-chosen)

2.01   T: 'Go to (Aux) and she will show you what you are going to colour in.'

Ryan has a photo-copied sheet of circles which he has to colour in. There is a tin of coloured pencils and another tin containing felt pens on the table. Aux suggests he chooses something to colour in the circles. He sits looking at the other boy and his own circles sheet for several moments before he starts – and then only after gentle prompting from Aux he starts to colour the large circle.

2.07   Aux moves away to speak to a child in another group. Ryan immediately stops colouring and looks round the room. It is becoming obvious that he has no interest in what he is doing and wants to be somewhere else. Aux returns and after more gentle persuasion he continues with his colouring in a very dilatory manner.

T arrives and looks at what he is doing. Suggests to Aux that he should do just the large circle and a smaller one rather than all of them on the sheet! He is to be encouraged to use the language – large, small, smaller, etc. applicable to his choice.

2.15   He is now only too obviously wanting to do something else. Aux is now keeping up a persuasive *running commentary* – 'Keep your eyes on your work – you're not looking – you're not doing it – come on you've nearly finished.'

He is using a red pencil to colour in the large circle and it is too fine for the large area he hs to colour.

T comes over to the table again and says he can do one of the small ones now. He chooses the smallest one.

2.20   Ryan finishes his small circle in a few seconds and is directed to the next activity.

Activity 3 (Ryan and Aux)

2.22   T: 'Go to (Aux) and paint the speckles on your frog.'

He finds his frog. Is asked by Aux to go and put an apron on which he does. Returns to table and puts some brown spots on the frog. He completes the speckles. Aux tells him to put the apron away and go and find out from the

teacher what he should do next.
He wanders across to put away his apron looking round the room as he does so.
He is in no hurry.

2.24   He goes to teacher who asks him to go across to partner helper who will help him to do more on his family book.

Activity 4 (4, 3b 1g; 4+; teacher-chosen)

2.25   Ryan arrives at the table. Parent shows him his book of his family. She shows him the pretend daddy page made from catalogue cut out pictures of a man labelled Daddy and arrows connecting him to three objects belonging to him. The ones he has chosen are – a camera, a boot, and another camera!
T tells him that today he is going to do his Mummy page.
She gives him a catalogue and he starts to slowly turn over the pages. He sits with his chin cupped in his hand and turns the pages over very slowly with his free hand.
She looks at him kindly and says 'Have you found one who looks a bit like your Mummy yet?'
Ryan shakes his head and goes on turning the pages but doesn't choose a picture.
He suddenly decides upon one which is fairly awkwardly placed near the spine of the catalogue. He tackles it very inexpertly and the Parent interjects with 'Watch what you are doing when you cut the top. I don't think Mummy wants her hair cut today!'
Ryan looks at her and laughs.
His speech is very indistinct and he mumbles something about mummy which neither the parent nor I can understand.
He completes his poor attempt at cutting out and is shown how to glue it and then where to place it on the page.
Parent is very relaxed and gentle with him. The other children in the group have completed the activity and left. She suggests he should now choose something that belongs to Mummy.
After some deliberation he decides upon a shoe. Parent says it is a good idea. He can't cut it properly and she suggests he may find it easier if he holds the paper with one hand while cutting with the other.

2.35   He stops cutting shoe before completing the task and is looking round the room. He is showing the same signs of lack of interest as before but is not displaying the restlessness as when he was colouring. He now starts to look for something else to put on the page. As he looks through the catalogue he discovers the toy pages. He immediately starts to peruse these with some interest. He tells Parent several toys which he has at home. She listens with interest and talks to him about them. She then gently suggests he should find another thing which belongs to Mummy.

2.40   He decides on a watch. He cuts it out without apparent care or interest. He frequently pauses and looks at the other children.
Parent: 'Now just one more thing for Mummy.'
He turns to the toy pages!
Parent: 'Ooh, does Mummy have toys?'
Ryan laughing: 'No, just me.'
Parent: 'Haven't your sisters got any toys, too?'
Ryan: 'Don't like theirs.'
Ryan then finds the kitchen equipment pages. He suggests in turn – kettle, toaster, washing machine, cooker. He then finds the bathroom page and suggests a shower!
To each of above Parent asks where it belongs. He replies correctly!
Parent then responds: 'Well that belongs in the ... not to Mummy.'
This process continues laboriously until he alights again on the toys! Parent produces a pile of detached catalogue sheets all of which depict a wide selection of female type accoutrements.
Ryan immediately chooses a page of necklaces and proceeds with great gusto to cut the page diagonally thus deftly managing to cut all the necklaces in half in one action!
Parent registers this with a look of anguish! 'Oh dear, Mummy's beads will have fallen all over the floor!'
This greeted with a chuckle from Ryan but the cutting did not falter. The remnants of two necklaces are stuck on to the page. She then asks where Ryan wants her to draw the arrows and how many she has to put?
Ryan: 'Two.'
Parent: 'Try again.'
Ryan after some deliberation: 'Three.'
Parent: 'Good boy now you have finished.'
Ryan rushes across room to wash the glue off his hands.

3.00   Teacher asks children to pack away their things and come over to the carpet area. 'We are going to sing and do the actions to Hokey Cokey. We'll all have some fun together.'

Activity 5 (12, 7b, 5g; 4+; teacher-chosen)

The adults and children are all doing the Hokey Cokey and all seem to be thoroughly enjoying it.
The song finishes and the girls are sent to get their coats.
Then the boys are asked to get their coats.

3.10   They return from the cloakroom area with their coats on. There are a few minutes left. T leads them in reciting the Cat and Mice rhyme. The children join in with enthusiasm.
They say 'good afternoon' and leave the room accompanied by the aux.

Interviews with child

Activity 1 Confirmed that Ryan did not understand the names of the shapes, and found the activity difficult.

Activity 2 Ryan did not enjoy this task which he found tedious and repetitive. He knew what a circle was.

Activity 3 Confirmed he knew what to do and did it easily and confidently.

Activity 4 He understood the requirements of the activity but found it difficult and did not enjoy it. Agreed his involvement was poor – said he wanted to play instead.

Activity 5 Enjoyed the song and did appropriate actions.

Interview with teacher

Did the child get out of this activity what you expected?

Activity 1 Yes, he volunteered to join in.

Activity 2 Yes. He needs a lot of practice with pencil control. He also needs to learn to finish something.

Activity 3 Yes, he has made a good job of his clay frog.

Activity 4 He was working with the parent helper and I didn't see him. (She is experienced and qualified and I don't interfere after I have set the activity.)

Activity 5 Yes he seemed to enjoy it, he certainly joined in.

Was it a success/failure?   Why?

Activity 1 Success – he joined in which is a step forward
Activity 2 Success – he coloured in all that was asked of him.
Activity 3 Yes – he has completed his frog satisfactorily.
Activity 4 Don't know yet.
Activity 5 Success – he joined in all the actions with fair accuracy and apparent enjoyment.

In the light of this what will you do next?

Activity 1 The introduction of these flat shapes is a fore-runner to 3D shapes next term.
Activity 2 Squares to be coloured in.
Activity 3 We are going to do a story about the Frog Prince.

Activity 4 He will do a page for each of his sisters next. He won't be doing it for a day or two, though.

Activity 5 More experience with action songs and rhymes.

Guidelines for discussion

1 i) Did the activities planned for Ryan match the teacher's intentions?
   ii) Would you have planned the same activities?

2 What do you think of the teacher's next intentions? Would you have planned different intentions? If so, why?

3 What was the role of the teacher, the auxiliary and parent helper in this session. How could the quality of any of the three be improved?

4 What did Ryan achieve in this session?

References

Anderson L M, Brubaker N L, Alleman-Brooks J and Duffy G G (1984) 'Making seatwork work'. IRT Research Series 142, Michigan State University.

Ausubel D K (1968) *Educational Psychology: A Cognitive View*. New York. Holt, Rinehart and Winston.

Barker Lunn J (1972) 'Length of infant school and academic performance'. *Educational Research* 14, 120–127.

Barrett G (1986) *Starting School: An Evaluation of the Experience*. CARE. University of East Anglia.

Bennett D (1987) 'The aims of teachers and parents for children in their first year at school'. In NFER/SCDC *Four Year Olds in School*. Windsor. NFER.

Bennett N, Desforges C, Cockburn A and Wilkinson B (1984) *The Quality of Pupil Learning Experiences*. London, Erlbaum Assoc.

Bennett N (1987) 'Cooperative Learning: children do it in groups – or do they?' *Educational and Child Psychology*, 3/4, 7–18.

Bennett N, Roth E, Dunne R (1987) 'Task processes in mixed and single age classes'. *Education 3–13*, 15, 43–50.

Bennett N (1988) 'The effective primary school teacher: the search for a theory of pedagogy'. *Teaching and Teacher Education*, 4, 19–30.

Bennett N and Desforges C (1988) 'Matching classroom tasks to students' attainments'. *Elementary School Journal*. 88, 221–234.

Bennett N and Cass A (1989) *Special to Ordinary: Case Studies in Integration*. London, Cassell (Forthcoming).

Bennett N and Wragg E C (1989) Primary Teacher Education, Leverhulme Research Programme. University of Exeter.

Bookbinder G E (1967) 'The preponderance of summer born children in ESN Classes: Which is responsible, age or length of infant schooling?' *Educational Research*, 9, 213–217.

Bruner J (1980) *Under Five in Britain*. London, Grant McIntyre.

Bruner J (1985) 'On teaching thinking: an afterthought'. In Chipman S F, Segal J W and Glaser R (Eds) *Thinking and Learning Skills Vol 2*. Hillsdale NJ, Erlbaum Assoc.

Bruner J and Haste H (Eds) (1987) *Making Sense*. London, Methuen.

Cashdan A and Meadows S (1983) *Teaching Styles in Nursery Education.* Final Report to SSRC. HR 3456.

Clark M M (1988) *Children under Five.* London, Gordon and Breach.

Cleave S, Jewett S and Bate M (1982) *And So to School*, Windsor, NFER–Nelson.

Cleave S, Barker-Lunn J and Sharp C (1985) 'Local education authority policy on admission to infant/first school'. *Educational research* 27, 40–43.

Curtis A M (1987) *A Curriculum for the Pre-School Child: Learning to Learn.* Windsor, NFER.

Department of Education and Science (1985) 'Better Schools'. *Education White Paper.* Cmnd 9469. London, HMSO.

Department of Education and Science (1987a) 'Pupils under five years in each local education authority in England. January, 1986'. *Statistical Bulletin 9/87.* London, DES.

Department of Education and Science (1987b) 'Pupil-teacher ratios for each Local Education Authority. January 1986'. *Statistical Bulletin 8/87.* London, DES.

Desforges C and Cockburn A (1987) *Understanding the Mathematics Teacher.* Falmer, London.

Dowling M (1988) *Education 3 to 5.* Paul Chapman Publishers, London.

Fogelman K and Gorbach P (1978) 'Age of starting school and attainment at eleven'. *Educational Research* 21, 65–6.

Galton M, Simon B and Croll P (1980) *Inside the Primary School.* London, RKP.

Her Majesty's Inspectorate (1978) *Primary Education in England.* London, HMSO.

Her Majesty's Inspectorate (1983) *9–13 Middle Schools: An Illustrative Survey.* London, HMSO.

Her Majesty's Inspectorate (1985) *Education 8–12 in Combined and Middle Schools.* London, HMSO.

Her Majesty's Inspectorate (1988) *The New Teacher in School.* London, HMSO.

House of Commons (1986) 'Achievement in Primary Schools', *Report of Select Committee on Education, Science and the Arts.* London, HMSO.

Hughes M, Pinkerton G and Plewis I (1979) 'Children's difficulties on starting infant school'. *Journal of Child Psychology and Psychiatry* 20, 187–196.

Hughes M, Mayall B, Moss P, Perry J, Petrie P and Pinkerton G (1980) *Nurseries Now.* Harmondsworth, Penguin.

Hughes M (1983) 'Teaching arithmetic to pre-school children'. *Educational Review* 35, 163–173.

Hutt S J, Tyler S, Hutt C and Foy H (1984) *A Natural History of the Pre-School.* Final Report to DES (quoted in Clark M (1988)).

James W (1899) *Talks to Teachers.* London, Longman Green.

Kellmer Pringle M L, Butler N and Davie R (1966) *11,000 Seven Year Olds.* London, Longman.

Kounin J S (1970) *Discipline and Group Management in Classrooms.* New York, Holt, Rinehart and Winston.

Lane S and Bergan J R (1988) 'Effects of instructional variables on language ability of pre-school children'. *American Educ. Res. J.* 25, 271–283.

Lemlech J K (1988) *Classroom Management.* London, Longman.

Mortimore P, Sammons P, Stoll L, Lewis D and Ecob R (1988) *School Matters.* Wells, Open Books.

Osborn A F (1981) 'Under fives in school in England and Wales 1971-9'. *Educational Research* 23, 96-103.

Osborn A F and Milbank J E (1987) *The Effects of Early Education.* Oxford, Clarendon Press.

Peel J (1988) 'The admission of four year old children to primary schools in Lancashire'. Paper presented at NFER conference on Starting School at Four: Planning for the Future, Solihull.

Perry J D, Guidubaldi J, Kehle T J (1979) 'Kindergarten competencies as predictors of third grade classroom behaviour and achievement'. *J. Educ. Psych.* 71, 443-450.

Plowden Report (1967) *Children and their Primary Schools.* London, HMSO.

Roehler L R, Duffy G G and Meloth M S (1983) 'The effects and some distinguishing characteristics of explicit teacher explanation during reading instruction'. Paper presented at National Reading Conference, Austin, Texas.

Russell R J H and Startup M (1986) 'Month of the birth and academic achievement'. *Personality and Individual Differences.* 7, 839-846.

Sestini E (1987) 'The quality of the learning experiences of four year olds in nursery and infant classes'. In NFER/SCDC *Four Year Olds in School.* Windsor, NFER.

Sharp C (1987) 'Starting school at four'. *Research Papers in Education.* 3, 64-90.

Slavin R E (1983) *Cooperative Learning.* New York, Longman.

Shulman L S (1986) Paradigms and research programs in the study of teaching: A contemporary perspective. In M C Wittrock (ed) *Handbook of Research on Teaching.* 3, 3-36, New York, Macmillan.

Staniland B (1986) 'Provision for the Under Fives in School'. Paper presented at DES Regional Conference: Education in the Early Years, Rolle College.

Stretzer R (1964) 'The origins of full time compulsory schooling at five'. *British Journal of Educational Studies.* 12, 16-28.

Sylva K, Roy C and Painter M (1980) *Child Watching at Playgroup and Nursery School.* London, Grant McIntyre.

Thomas I (1987) 'The Bedfordshire 4+ pilot scheme: some issues and implications': In NFER/SCDE *Four Year Olds in School.* Windsor, NFER.

Tizard B (1985) 'Social relationships between adults and young children, and their impact on intellectual functioning'. In Hinde R A, Perret-Clermont, A N, Stevenson-Hinde J (Eds). *Social Relationships and Cognitive Development.* Oxford, Oxford University Press.

Tizard B, Blatchford, P, Burke J, Farquhar C, and Plewis I (1988) *Young Children at School in the Inner City,* London, Erlbaum Ass.

Topping K (1988) *The Peer Tutoring Handbook.* London, Croom Helm.

Tyler S, Foy H and Huff C (1979) 'Attention and activity in the young child'. *Brit. J. Educ. Psych.* 49, 194-197.

Vygotsky L S (1962) *Thought and Language.* New York, Wiley.

Weir R (1988) 'Some elements of current practice'. Paper presented at NFER conference on Starting School at Four: Planning for the Future, Solihull.

Wood D, McMahan L and Cranstoun Y (1980) *Working with Under Fives.* London, Grant McIntyre.

Wood D (1988) *How Children Think and Learn,* Oxford, Blackwell.

Woodhead M (1989) 'School starts at 5 ... or 4 years old? The rationale for changing admission policy in England and Wales'. *Journal of Education Policy,* 4, 1-22.

Appendix

Class Teacher – Interview Schedule

1 Class teacher | M | | F |

    Age range trained for   [   ]

    Post of responsibility   [   ]

    Area of responsibility   . . . .

    Number of years teaching 1st year children   [ ]

    Number of years in teaching   [ ]

    Preferred age group   [ ]

    Previous experience with 4 year olds*   [ ]

    Number of years teaching 4 year olds*   [ ]

    Probationer   [ ]

*   younger than rising fives

2 Size of class   Autumn Term   [ ]

    Age range of class (in years and months)   [   ]

    Number of 4 year olds (including rising 5s)   [ ]

Number of 1st years (statutory school age) ☐

Number of 2nd years ☐

Number of 3rd years ☐

Auxiliary help | NNEB | C.Ass | Y | N |

Auxiliary help – average hours per day

Mon ☐

Tues ☐

Wed ☐

Thurs ☐

Fri ☐

Parental help – average hours per day

Mon ☐

Tues ☐

Wed ☐

Thurs ☐

Fri ☐

What kind of help do the auxiliaries provide?

....

....

....

What kind of help do the parents provide?

....

....

....

Others (students etc)

....

....

3   Classroom context

Do you think you have sufficient space for the
number of children in your class?

Autumn	Y	N
Spring	Y	N
Summer	Y	N

Number of rooms/areas

How many of these are shared?

Number of areas for exclusive use of 4 year olds

Are these: permanent?

      temporary?

Accessibility of: toilets — Easy | Diff

      cloakrooms — Easy | Diff

      outdoor play area — Easy | Diff

Is there: carpet area? — Y | N

      practical area? — Y | N

      quiet book area? — Y | N

      water supply? — Y | N

      display area? — Y | N

Are there any other facilities for the exclusive use
of the 4 year olds each term? — Y | N

If so, what are they?

....

....

....

4   Are you consulted about the financial provision for
      your class? | Y | | N |

      Are you satisfied with the provision of equipment
      and teaching resources in your classroom? | Y | | N |

      If NO – list your needs in order of priority:

....

....

....

5   Organisation of the classroom

      On what basis do you group the children in your class?

                                          age   [   ]

                                          friendship [   ]

                                          ability   [   ]

                                          mixed ability [   ]

      Do you integrate the 4 year olds into these groups? | Y | | N |

      If YES, how?

....

....

....

If NO, what do you do?
  and why?

....

....

....

....

....

Are they likely to stay in these groups throughout
the year? | Y | | N |

If NO, how will they change?

....

....

....

....

....

6   How do you structure the learning programme for your
    class?

....

....

....

....

....

Is this different for the 4 year olds in the class? | Y | | N |

If YES, how does it differ?

....

....

....

....

....

Does each intake of 4 year olds get the same programme? | Y | | N |

If YES

How do you cope with the scope of the programme with the children who will only have 1 or 2 terms in their 1st year of schooling?

....

....

....

....

....

If NO

How do you choose which part of the programme to give them?

....

....

....

....

....

7   What are your main curricular priorities for the 4 year
     olds?

     ....

     ....

     ....

     ....

8   From your experience what are the major problems, if any,
     that you face in teaching 4 year olds?

     ....

     ....

     ....

     ....

9   Have you a particular philosophy regarding the education
     of 4 year olds?

     ....

     ....

     ....

     Do you find that you are able to implement it in your
     classroom?

     ....

     ....

10   Have you any other comments on teaching 4 year olds in
     school?

Head Teacher – Interview Schedule

Overview of school

1 Type of school

First ☐

Combined ☐

Infant ☐

Primary ☐

Nursery unit ☐

2 Size of school

No of pupils ☐

Staffing   H+ ☐

Teaching Head ☐

Contact time with 4 year olds per week ☐ hrs

Non-teaching staff allocation throughout the school

....

....

....

Parental help in school

....

....

....

Desirable class size for 4 year olds ☐

3 Head teacher

M	F

Length of time in post

Age range trained for

Preferred age group

Is there a scale post for early years?

Is this held by one of the teachers of the 4 year olds?

4 Location of school

....

....

....

Socio-economic background of parents

....

....

....

5 Admissions

Number of intakes per year

	i pt	pt	ft
Number of 4 year olds admitted: Autumn			
Project number of 4 year olds to Spring			
be admitted Summer			

Age range of 4 year olds admitted each intake
  (in years and months)

6 Structure of 1st year class/es throughout first year of school

Number of classes with 4 year olds	Autumn	☐
	Spring	☐
	Summer	☐

Class size/s (actual)	Autumn	☐	☐
Class size/s (projected)	Spring	☐	☐
Class size/s (projected)	Summer	☐	☐
Number of 4 year olds in each class	Autumn	☐	☐
(projected)	Spring	☐	☐
(projected)	Summer	☐	☐
Age range of 1st year classes each term	Autumn	☐	☐
	Spring	☐	☐
	Summer	☐	☐

7 Admission procedure

home visits:	☐
toy/book/story club: for pre-school children	☐
Individual informal visits to school: parents	☐
parents with child	☐
Individual visits with formal interviews: parents	☐
parents with child	☐

Other contact

....

8 Liaison
(In the context of the 4 year olds)
     Playgroup on site

     Liaison with: playgroup

         nursery unit or class

         health visitors

         social workers

         other agencies   . . . .

   . . . .

Do you fill in a county admission form? | Y | N |

Is your admission procedure stated in the school's booklet? | Y | N |

9 Is there any particular financial provision that you
are able to make for this age group? | Y | N |

What is it for the current school year?

. . . .

. . . .

. . . .

. . . .

How is it funded?

. . . .

. . . .

. . . .

. . . .

(Probe for capitation and other sources of finance)

10 Have you got a particular philosophy regarding the education
of the 4 year old in school? Are you able to implement it?

....

....

....

....

....

11 Does the education of this group of children present a
problem in your school?

....

....

....

....

....

12 What are your views about this LEA's admission policy and
terms of provision?

....

....

....

....

....

13 Is there any difference in the quality of educational
experience that the children receive in each of the intake
terms?

....

....

....

....

....

14 Any further comments?

....

....

....

....